ALL &
BEYOND

FLAMENCO

First published in September 2024 by

FLAMENCO

Copyright © 2024 Thomas Dolan

No part of this book may be reproduced
in any form without permission from
the Publisher, except for the quotation
of brief passages in criticism

Cover Illustration & Book Design: Neil Hague

**British Library Cataloguing-in
Publication Data**
A catalogue record for this book is
available from the British Library

ISBN 978-1-3999-7972-6

ALL & BEYOND

THOMAS DOLAN

Dedication:

This book is dedicated to all those who have suffered, are suffering and will suffer for the sake of truth, and all the victims of so-called satanic forces.

Contents (Index)

Preface	1
Introduction	3
CHAPTER 1	5
CHAPTER 2	7
CHAPTER 3	9
CHAPTER 4	12
CHAPTER 5	14
CHAPTER 6	17
CHAPTER 7	20
CHAPTER 8	23
CHAPTER 9	26
CHAPTER 10	27
Acting	28
Action and Reaction	28
Alertness	29
Arrogance	29
Art	30
Attention	31
Authority	31
Avoiding Radical Solutions	32
Belief	34
Boredom	36

Cogitation and Thought	37
Compassion	38
Competition	38
Conspiracies	39
Control	39
Shifting Focus	46
The Pyramid of Psychological Control	47
Creation and Free Will	48
The Illusion of All Possibilities and the Concept of Time	49
Death	53
Demons and Human Suffering	53
Discipline	56
Discussion and Argument	56
Dreams	56
Education	60
Elite	60
Emotions	61
Establishments	62
Caretakers	63
Quangos	63
The Last Freedom	64
Eroticism and Pornography	64
Evil Eye	65
Evolution	65
Faith, Hope, Charity and Trust	66
Fear and Morbidity	67
Fictional Justice	69
Forgiveness	69
Freedom	70
God	71
Guilt	73

Healing	75
Heaven and Hell	77
Humanity	78
Humility and Learning	79
Identity	80
Images, Labels, Words and Subliminal Control	81
Imperceptibility	82
Impulses, Urges and Music	83
Innocence	84
Intellect and Intelligence	85
Interpretation, Humour and Laughter	86
Introspection	87
Judgement	88
Karma, Crime and Punishment	88
Laws	95
Logic	95
Love	96
Magic	98
Masculinity and Femininity	99
Meaning	100
Meditation and Revelation	100
Memory	101
Misconceptions	102
Money	105
Morbidity and the Psyche	108
Mysteries	109
Need, Wanting and Giving	110
Paedophilia	111
Peace of Mind	113
Personality and Character	113
Pleasure	113
Possession by Demons	113
Possessiveness	114
Prayer	114

Problems	115
Psyche and Personality	115
Psychology and Psychiatry	116
Race	117
Reawakening to Full Consciousness	119
Real Values	135
Relics	136
Religion	136
Science	137
Self-remembering	138
Sexuality and Sex	138
Sincerity	143
States, Qualities, Conditions, Mind and Psyche ...	143
Suffering	144
Superthought	145
Talent	146
Time, Space and Motion	146
The Pendulum and its relation to Gravity, Time, Weight and Measurement	147
How the Pendulum Functions	148
Clock Time	148
Psychological Time	149
Time, Perception and Age	151
Time Travel	153
The Magic of Free Will	153
Truth and Permanence	154
Veils	155
Violence	156
War	157
Yoga	162
Relaxation	163
Slow Motion	163
Breathing	164
Visualization	164

Astral Projection	166
Doing Without Trying	167
Effort and Energy	167
Forestalling Negative Events	167
Visual Memory	168
Kundalini	168
Pendulum Control of Rhythms	169
Sonics	169
Directing Energy	170
Inner Awareness	170
Melding	170
Raising and Lowering Vibrations	171
Doing the Impossible	171
A Final Word	174

About The Author

Born in Dublin, Ireland, Thomas relocated to London, England, and worked as a skilled joiner by trade. Everything he took an interest in he would learn about to the ninth degree. Anyone who knew him would describe him as highly knowledgeable and the life of the party, but always humble and kind. He seemed to see everything for what it was and told it how it was too. There are many who spoke with him about spiritualism, consciousness, mysticism, demonology and other subjects in his lifetime, but very few were aware of his origin, alluded to in the preface of this book.

With access to 'consciousness', he began collating ideas for this book and expounding those ideas into the public domain at a young age. He had many experiences that could be described as 'supernatural', or what many others achieved through meditation, astral projection, past life regression, chemically induced experiences and so on. Towards the end of his life, he regularly worked on finished manuscript you are about to read, combing it for errors or inaccuracies. Sadly he died in 2022.

PREFACE

It is true, you only live once, but you dream many times. You are now in one of those dreams. You are temporarily trapped in a wheel of karma, which consists of many dreams, some pleasant, some not. Only you can decide when these dreams end and you reawaken to reality. Reality is the eternal now. The concept of time only exists in your dreams.

Heaven does exist. It is the reality you will know when you finally finish dreaming. Purgatory and limbo only exist in or on the periphery of your dreams. Your dreams are not any kind of test or game. Each one represents an opportunity to wake up to reality. In order to wake, you must learn about the dream to find your way out. These dreams, which you call lives, are governed by how deeply you are involved in the automatic thought process.

The best description of the concept of hell would be to have a glimpse of heaven, and know you would never see it again.

There is the stillness of supreme consciousness.

There is the stirring of that stillness.

The stirring creates opposites from the neutrality of nothingness.

The attraction between the separated opposites creates laws of nature.

The resulting creation consists of the free will of consciousness.

The stirring of free will creates all possibilities.

There is complete silence. In the blackness of space, earth floats gracefully in the cushion of its atmosphere. The ball of the sun floats a long way off, but its rays of energy blend with earth's atmosphere, creating new life on the surface below. One horizon swings easily into the warm light of day, while the other rolls endlessly into night. As you draw nearer to this ball of light and darkness, you are headed for the lighted side. Gradually, the blackness around you begins to lighten, until you are engulfed in the life-giving atmosphere.

You glide in through the white mist and soon begin to discern colours. The atmosphere around you takes on a breathtakingly beautiful shade of light blue, with deeper blues, greys and greens below. You veer to the right and head for the dark side. Masses of land and water fly past below, as the light blue around you turns to purple. You slow down and hover above a city. A hundred feet below is a street of grey slate rooftops with a row of brick chimneys. Although it is night in this place you are aware of every detail in this part of the city.

You absorb the vibrations and sense that something has got here before you, something not quite right. Without further hesitation you fall in a left-hand spiral through the slates and into the body of an infant in a cot.

INTRODUCTION

You think everything is just fine. You are a reasonably good person trying your best, in a reasonably good society trying its best, in a reasonably good world trying its best. Just a few minor problems here and there. The odd villain. Human nature, the experts tell you. Well, you can't argue with the experts, you are told. They know. Anyway the villains always get their just deserts. That's what the legal system is for. So you don't have to bother your head with that one. Your life is full and you are busy looking out for you and yours. You accept what you see, hear and read in the news media. You don't believe it all but it makes it easier to accept when there it all is in black and white. That makes it official. Millions of your fellow human beings are being murdered, forced into slavery, tortured or starved to death in filth and disease. This could be you tomorrow, but as long as it is not you today you turn a blind eye. Anyway, that is the business of other people in other countries. The experts tell you they brought it all on themselves, but, just in case you have a twinge of conscience, they have a system in place they call charity, where you can buy peace of mind. That makes it easier to forget that there is something terribly wrong with the social structures of the planet. But they have a system in place whereby all and sundry can be explained away by carefully selected individuals they call experts. So everything is fine? Think again. There are very important issues to be investigated, but a lot of unimportant trivia has to be cleared out of the way in order to establish a clear starting point for a sincere enquiry into aspects of life which really do matter. There is something extraordinary out there, not physically out there but beyond the narrow scope of the mind in its present condition. Only known facts are stated here and no amount of disbelief will ever alter that. This is not about localised chaos, hunting down villains, the games people play, the nonsense of any religion, preachers who deliberately stop short of the truth, justifying or judging. It is about the condition of the human mind here and now, and the possibility of a mind freeing itself by finding its true identity.

Who are you?
What are you?

If you already know who and what you are, you need not read any further, but if there is the slightest doubt, read on.

CHAPTER ONE

Prepare yourself for some shocking information. It is shocking because it is true.

What you have always accepted as the real you is in fact not the real you at all. The real you is not a D.N.A. structure. The real you is a totally free spiritual being which has become trapped in a world created by an ancient race of beings.

The real you has allowed itself to be tempted into the denser realms of astral sensations and thence lulled to sleep. The trap consists of a purely mechanical device constructed from thoughts and words, a thought-machine, an extremely sophisticated virtual reality machine developed through various aspects of time.

This is the dreaming you. Do you wish to wake from the dream? If so, read on.

Your mind is your own. The thoughts which occupy it are not. This is a fact. But it is not good enough to simply state that. It must be seen to be true beyond all possible doubt; otherwise the initial statement would be pointless. What you perceive as your thoughts are in fact drowning out the inner silence of the mind, which is your true identity, the real you. In order to fully appreciate this, it is necessary to become acquainted with the workings of the thought process, and evolve beyond it. Only then can you really know who and what you are.

Much has been said and written about the problems of living on this planet. These problems have existed for thousands of years. Billions of individuals have been murdered, tortured, starved, worked to death, while certain individuals have glibly promised 'a better tomorrow'.

Millions of these tomorrows have come and gone but none of them have been any better. Why is this? What is going on? What is it all about? Why have some individuals assumed the right to tell others how they should live their lives? Have they stumbled on some great secret that has somehow stayed hidden from others? Why have all the wise men failed to make a better world? Is there a communication problem? Are the wise men really wise? Are they all liars, or just some? Who are the charlatans?

A great proportion of what has been written about the meaning of life has been the product of confused minds. A smaller proportion has been written with intent to deceive the gullible reader. Almost none of what has been written can be regarded as a serious enquiry into anything. It is true that serious works have been written but they are in the minority and need to be sought like the proverbial needle in a haystack. In the past, serious works on the subject have been sought out and destroyed. The books and those who wrote or possessed them were ritualistically burned as a warning to others. Whether a work is serious or not, it is what the reader makes of it that really matters. Many people read nonsense and feel greatly enriched by it. Many read a serious work and throw it away after struggling through half a page. In truth, a work is written and that is where the matter ends. It is up to the reader after that. It does not matter in the least who takes it seriously. Like a grain of sand it simply exists. The spoken word may be twisted or forgotten, but the written word remains in its original form, giving every reader the same message.

Some books are written poetically, to please the reader. These are merely a lullaby to soothe the sleeping infant. Some are written psychologically, to interest the reader. These are merely a game to amuse the child. If an enquiry is to be serious there are no lullabies or games. A serious enquiry does not proceed on an infantile level. It goes beyond the trivial, and appeals to that in the reader which is serious. It proceeds on solid ground, free of negative emotions, misconceptions and bias. It proceeds in accordance with logic. If the application of logic is not maintained, the enquiry immediately ends, and all further efforts become an aimless drudge until the application of logic is again established.

Poetry in itself is perfectly fine as a method of getting across a message in as few words as possible, but some messages require a more long-winded explanation. There are only two ways you can live your life. Either your mind controls the thought process, or the thought process controls your mind. If you are happy to surrender your true identity to the thought machine, don't bother to read any further.

CHAPTER TWO

The human being is not just a body with a brain in the head. The complete being consists of body-brain, mind-super mind, and spirit. The body and brain are one organic unit, basically chemical, but infused with the natural electricity of the life force. The brain is the control centre, the engine of the vehicle. The sole function of the brain is to maintain the body in full health. The organic unit is earthbound, coming from and returning to the earth. The brain cannot truly think or cogitate. It is controlled by the mind.

The mind, although part of the whole human being, is not earthbound. It is electrical and infuses the organic unit with the life force. Since electricity has the power to change chemical structures the mind has full control over the organic unit (mind over matter). While the physical aspect is alive and functioning, the mind is connected to it but has the ability to stretch itself anywhere in the thought-field or astral plane, as they call it. At the same time it always remains with the body, for which it is responsible. It is the sacred function of the mind to cogitate freely. It can fully appreciate the beauty of planetary life through the physical senses. It is the true identity of the human being, the point of sane balance, the beginning of the journey to full consciousness.

The supermind comes into being if and when the mind chooses to cleanse itself of the thought-process and elevate itself to a vibratory level which becomes invisible to the world of thought. It becomes untouchable. It cogitates faster than the speed of light. It can sense a flash of lightning in an instant before it materializes. It is the ultimate state of alertness, the ever remembering guardian of the mind.

The spirit, which cannot be described in words, is literally beyond anything the mind can conceive. The beauty of the spirit is infinitely beyond any attempt at description and infinitely beyond that again. It is what they call nirvana. To the mind which seeks truth for truth's sake the notion of any one individual attaining these heights while leaving the rest of humanity in darkness and pain is ridiculous beyond words. All are one, and all knowledge has to be shared or all existence would have no meaning.

The body is the vehicle.

The brain is the engine.

The mind is the knowledge which fuels the brain.

The spirit allows the mind to have that knowledge.

If the mind maintains conscious contact with the spirit all will be well. If the mind loses such conscious contact, a psyche, which is no more than an unwitting agent of a hopelessly insane astral or thought entity may push the mind to one side and take control of the vehicle. In this case all will not be well.

You are capable of reaching these heights. All it takes is the determination of a sincere mind and the first step. Those who are not acquainted with this subject will find it very strange territory, but hopefully will come to grasp its importance.

CHAPTER THREE

The mind is born into its own world. It shares the planet with other minds also born into their own worlds. Same planet, different worlds. The first period of infancy is fully automatic. The mind slowly wakes to the new environment. At this point the mind is untainted by the thought-process, due to the fact that as yet there is no build-up of memories and their associations to cloud or hinder pure cogitation. During this initial period of adjustment the mind receives impulses through the brain from the physical senses. It hears sounds, feels different surface textures, smells different tastes and sees light patterns and movement. There is also a definite sense of self, as opposed to the perceived phenomena. The mind watches and waits for it all to make sense. The infant is picked up by its parents and there is a sense of vulnerability in the hands of these mysterious beings. There is a vague awareness that certain routines are being followed on a regular basis. The drudgery continues day after day. The mind begins to differentiate between day and night routines. In the light of day it experiences through its senses. In the darkness of night it is left alone with its awareness, temporarily free from the incessant daily routine with all its noise and fuss. It has its first memories of daily events.

These memories are not accompanied by associations, as yet. They are just pure memories. As the child gets older, the dark and peace of night become a time for thinking, thoughts of the day's events and other new thoughts. These new thoughts are the sole property of the young mind. The days go by and the memories build up, --indicate an accepted form of behaviour. At night the mind pushes these memories aside to make room for the new and more interesting thoughts. When the awareness is broken down to the basic level, what is left is real knowing, as the thing known does not depend on any external data or influences. It can see clearly from its centre of silence. This is the beginning of true, independent cogitation. The mind begins to enquire.

The first 'whys' come into being. The mind is not yet conditioned, as there is not enough build-up of associative memories. So, from this clear starting point logic can be applied without the encroachment of any form of bias. The mind begins its first, tentative journeys into the mind itself, a land of never-ending adventures and possibilities, and the jungle of the encroaching thought-field. The mind knows its own true identity and is totally silent and attentive. It functions on spontaneous impulses. Its only food is knowing. It is in harmony with itself and all it perceives. It is without conflict, as conflict only arises in the thought-field when there is a build-up of conflicting input. The young mind comes to realise that it can look at the thought-process, and knows that the observing mind has got nothing whatsoever to do with that process. It can be seen clearly that the mind and the thought-process are two entirely different aspects of some greater totality.

To begin with, it looks at and studies the thought-process. Then it realises it can step outside itself and observe itself watching the thought-process. This creates three separate aspects:

1 – The whole thought-process.

2 – The mind watching the thought-process

3 – The silence watching the mind watching thought.

This third aspect of the totality becomes the watchdog, or guardian of the mind, and is the beginning of the state of alertness. It becomes the overseer of true cogitation. Thought is a process. Cogitation is not a process. It is the state of knowing without any involvement with thought. It cannot be touched by thought. The thought-process can only enter a mind and not the guardian of that mind.

How can the thought-process invade or take over the mind? Without the guardian, the mind is vulnerable. It is at the mercy of an encroaching, ever increasing army of thoughts and their attendant, associative memories, the inbuilt impulses of inherited traits, and all the brutal conditioning of the local environment. The child asks questions of its parents but only gets conditioned responses in return. So in the face of a futile situation all further enquiries will be introspective. At this early stage in the life of the mind, there are two possibilities. The mind can either choose to continue serious enquiry or turn its full attention to, and become immersed in the world of the physical. It has the free will to abandon the search for truth. If it does the latter it becomes involved with the thought-process, and slowly, imperceptibly, it becomes an individual thought-field within the greater process, a mere wheel within the machine. At this point it falls

under the influence of three automatic processes.
These are;

1 – The fixed, automatic chain of events within the local environment, or laws of nature.

2 – The inbuilt impulses of heredity.

3 – The brutal conditioning processes of the society or cult into which it was born.

4 – The most powerful are the laws of nature.

5 – The next most powerful are the inbuilt hereditary impulses or traits.

6 – The least powerful are the social influences.

Owing to the nature of these influences they are always in conflict. As yet, the young mind is only influenced by the first two. The third comes later.
When a young mind is taken over by the thought-process it becomes an integral part of the whole process which reaches far beyond the narrow scope of the mind's awareness of the thought- field in which it finds itself. The life of such a mind consists of being born, proceeding automatically in accordance with a set pattern of events brought about by many seen and unseen laws of mechanical nature, being bogged down by inherited reactions, emotions, social concepts etc. And finally dying after a life of confusion and conflict, none the wiser.
When a mind focuses its full attention on any concept, it actually becomes that which is at the point of focus. The unconscious path becomes totally submerged in thought and descends into confusion, thrashing about in its own tiny personal illusion, a world not created by itself but by external influences. Such a mind is easily manipulated by those influences. This mind is totally unaware of the manipulators.

CHAPTER FOUR

When consciousness is chosen, the mind, which has seen the thought process for what it is, has already disarmed the influence of heredity, thus taking control of its own life. At a later stage it will disarm the influence of social conditioning, and later still has the possibility of disarming even the fixed laws of nature. (See Magic) Consciousness is totally without conflict. It is freedom born of responsibility. It is not any kind of 'reward', as the concept of reward does not exist in reality. It is just a present state of being, flowing from the original decision to remain conscious. Life becomes an amazing succession of revelations, states of being unimaginable in the world of thought. New arrivals on the planet are at a tremendous disadvantage. Important knowledge is deliberately withheld from them. Vital knowledge which was their birth right, was withdrawn from the public domain into the hands of the few over centuries.

This knowledge is being used against the masses of humanity because of the morbid mind-set or psyche of a cluster of thought-entities evolved over eons. The human race has been kept in a condition of confused ignorance. All the new mind has to go by is its own individual ability to cogitate clearly at an early stage, and strive to see the truthful meaning of things before it becomes swallowed up by the thought-process which is predatory by nature. The mind either educates itself or it does not. The free mind explores every avenue of possibility. It not only observes the thought- process but can fully understand its mechanical nature and all the automatic processes involved. The mind, which has surrendered its true identity to the machine is open to all influences, and believes it has no choice but to obey. All this nonsense fills the mind which has chosen the belief system.

What is belief?

Belief is the acceptance of unproven data. To put it simply, the believer just cannot be bothered to seek the truth of any situation, and is fully prepared to live with any lie that fits the bill. This mind is no more or less than a cog on a wheel of the machine, a link in a chain of reactions which reaches away and out of sight. (*See* Action and Reaction)

There is the silent clear mind and there is the mind which has forgotten its true identity and become a mere psyche.

What is the psyche?

A psyche is the end result of an evolved thought-field which has stagnated and become totally fixed in its pattern of behaviour. It is totally predictable, like a machine where you press a certain button and you know exactly what the end result is going to be. This is precisely how the individual is manipulated. In this world all concepts of heaven and hell are merely a blip within the greater, ever-expanding, ever-changing illusion of all possibilities which invent and manufacture themselves, and leave no part of the imagination untouched. It gives birth to all good, bad and indifferent aspects. The mind is trapped in this mulch.

The awareness of the individual psyche is very limited. It can only sense an infinitesimal part of the total. Beyond this narrow perception is an ocean of thought-entities. The human psyche is being manipulated by the very worst elements imaginable. These predatory psyches wallow in every kind of depravity. There are only two ways to live your life. As a free mind, or as an automaton, or robot.

The robot is easily controlled from other realms. Events on earth are manipulated by these clowns. Earth is their playground and human beings are their toys.

CHAPTER FIVE

There are many positive aspects to people's lives, but their overall attempt at positive living is hindered every step of the way by the overwhelming number of negative aspects. At an early age in the life of the new mind, it is separated from its parents for the purpose of further conditioning. The young mind can see clearly how totally different each family atmosphere is, and how children are removed from their natural environment to be placed in the general mulch, like a universal recipe to fit the state's requirements, and create a generation gap in one fell swoop. They are told it is good for the children to 'mix' – to get a 'balanced personality (*See* Personality).

This is totally untrue. Complete nonsense. The child gains balance within the family circle, and can still mix naturally without being sent to an institution of conditioning. In these institutions, the child becomes alienated from its parents, and is exposed to every predatory mind-set and already conditioned psyche. The society, or state at large, steps in to take over the conditioning process, as independent-minded parents cannot be trusted to toe the state line.

This is done on the pretext of giving the 'lucky' child what they like to call 'education'. But the bare bones of the thing is that the state is 'legally kidnapping' the child, in order to remove it from the cocoon of family life. This is the thin end of the wedge, designed to create a 'generation-gap' and bring the child's mind into line with whatever the state requires, regardless of what the parents think. The tender young mind is snatched, and thrown into an ocean of conflicting nonsense. A school is no more than a children's prison. The battering and traumatising process continues until the state is satisfied that the young victim has become part of their corrupt system. What a neat set-up! The parents are not even aware that their child has been kidnapped. Now the young mind is in the vice-like grip of heredity, the state, and the laws of nature. But the young mind, which has been looking at the loose ends, and seeking the causes of this strange situation, will not be fooled by any of this nonsense. It sees through the lies of society. It sees the dirty streets, the crime, the injustice, the corruption, the poverty, and all the nonsense born of the thought-control system.

The question arises, -- It can't be an accident, so who or what is behind all this insanity? There is obviously no logic to any of it, just millions of wasted lives (*See* Karma). Any brave soul who stood up and spoke out against it was brutally murdered, their memory besmirched. The mind can see that there is something more sinister involved, when there is such imbalance in the distribution of all the earth has to offer. A vast, unstable planetary mess, organised chaos, controlled from a point beyond the human senses. All life on the physical level is controlled from the thought-field, or astral plane. Every physical action is first instigated in the mind. If that mind is silent it gives rise to sane, logical functioning of the physical, which is pure action. If that mind is filled with thoughts, there can be no sane functioning, no action, only reaction.

The enquiring mind can see through the false smiles, the empty promises and the beastly life-styles. These organisers of so-called societies are highly secretive in what they claim to be a free, open society. No outsiders are allowed to contribute in any way to their decision making, -- no members of the very society they claim to represent. 'Well' they say, 'You elected us to be your law-makers!' Most definitely not true. The really wholesome types the people would just love to elect have always been silenced through coercion, blackmail and murder. But don't dare try to prove it, - you can achieve more alive. Party politics is no more and no less than a cheap card-trick! Pick a card, any card, - but it must be this one! These fiends have numerous secret meetings, glorified feasts, where they gorge themselves on the decorated flesh of murdered beings they call animals, slap each other on the back, sexually abuse the children of local 'peasants', and display a look of 'everything's going according to plan' on their smug, overfed faces. While this stream of highly organised bestiality goes on, millions of humans are starving to death in filth and disease. These monsters steadily pump out 'reasons' why these people are starving.

There are psyches out there, so debased and perverted they are way beyond human comprehension. The whole of their world is based solely on the denial of truth. They are caught in an illusory emptiness, a void so terrible they need perpetual, mindless violence to drown out even the very remotest possibility of having to face the terrible limbo of nothingness. These creatures of the astral know no peace. When a human mind allows itself to enter this whispering, beckoning minefield of thought-traps, it immediately becomes a victim of these demons, these predators, The most horrific crimes known to humanity are perpetrated, not for any monetary gain, but purely and simply to inflict the absolute maximum mental and physical suffering on the victims, through physical and mental torture, and the fear of that torture.

The psyches which commit these crimes are of two types —

1 – A psyche direct from the astral plane which has taken up residence in a planetary mind, and operates directly through the physical body to commit the crimes (*See* possession).

2 – A planetary psyche which has been influenced by these demons.

So why do these demons do what they do? What do they gain? Every thought gives off or emits a 'cloud' of vibrations. These vibrations are an exact reflection of the thought which initiated them. If you think an 'angry' thought, it emits a cloud of 'angry' vibrations. Every emotion emits a cloud of vibrations which exactly mirrors that emotion. So if an angry emotion emits a certain strength of vibrations, a 'slightly annoyed' emotion emits a far weaker intensity of vibrations. A thought containing 'a great rage' gives off powerful, high-intensity ones, much more powerful than mere anger. If you accidently hit your thumb, or stub your toe, it gives off extremely high intensity vibrations. The more you suffer physically or mentally with any kind of stress or pain, the more powerful the emissions. Disembodied demons on the astral can 'taste' your pain-vibrations. Demons do not have a 'shape', as such. They are thought-forms. They thrive on the suffering of humans. It is their only food, their staple diet. Their one and only aim is to cause as much suffering as possible, and feed on it. The human race is perfect for this purpose. The planet earth is their farm and the human race is their main crop. These creatures have brought crop-intensive farming to a fine art. (*See* Race).

CHAPTER SIX

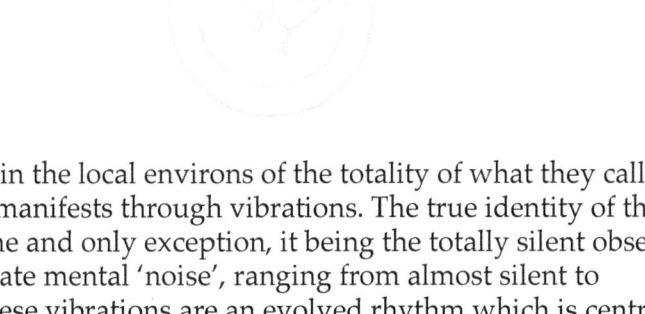

Everything in the local environs of the totality of what they call 'creation' manifests through vibrations. The true identity of the mind is the one and only exception, it being the totally silent observer. Vibrations create mental 'noise', ranging from almost silent to deafening. These vibrations are an evolved rhythm which is central to the whole of the local environment, giving rise to mathematics, music, and the full range of sensory perceptions. Thus the earth is governed, along with all its seen and unseen environs, by this 'sacred rhythm'. One of the great officially-encouraged misconceptions is that the human race is the only known form of intelligent life. This has always been a colossal lie.

To begin with, human beings are not physical beings, but originate from 'beyond the astral'. They come from a reality far beyond the understanding of anything within the astral. Human beings are temporarily 'trapped' within the astral plane of illusory thought-forms. If enough individuals free themselves from the thought-process, the 'chain of events' will break down, and there will be a new beginning to life on earth. All this may seem rather far-fetched, even crazy, but is, in fact, absolutely true. Individuals believe, accept blindly, far more crazy notions every day of their lives, unsuspecting, even for a moment, how they are being made fools of. (*See* Misconceptions).

There are many questions asked, such as, – how did it all begin? Why did it all begin? Right now, asking these questions is like trying to get on to a high roof by starting at the top rung of the ladder. If there is to be a journey, you don't begin from some distant point beyond your understanding. If you don't understand the question, you certainly won't understand the answer. You can be told any lie and you won't be any the wiser.

The journey begins here and now, from where you are, and with what you have, and what you know, actually truly know, however little. Evolution within the known astral world and that vast ocean beyond, can be compared to a large continent in a vast, endless ocean. It is populated by a given number of individuals, with an equal number of either sex. These beings include every type of psyche, good, bad, and indifferent. They see the ocean but do not understand it. There is much more than enough to sustain life. The requirement to respect and preserve the land, so that it continues to support life, is absolutely minimal. The land is incredibly beautiful, a paradise. Among the population, many automatic processes begin. Similar types will be drawn together. Different types will repel each other. The more cunning will easily outwit, and come to dominate the less cunning. Small groups will form. This fermentation process will continue automatically and affect every life. Some individuals will help the less fortunate. Some will deceive and corrupt, will even kill. Murder will become commonplace. The vast majority will be reduced to slavery. Confusion will reign. Emotion will take the place of logical reasoning. Hatred will rule in the absence of love. Corrupt activity will even affect plant-life, and the land will deteriorate.

The deliberate breeding of bad seed will be encouraged, both openly and in secret. The original good seed will become rarer. Violence will become the accepted norm. Perverted experiments with chemicals and artificial electricity will cause physical damage on a great scale. The population will give birth to brain-damaged and confused young. Many of these young will grow to so-called adulthood and give birth to even more damaged and confused young. The mutant seed will multiply and overrun the land. Confusion will be deemed normal. All through this process, the original, disruptive influences will have interbred, and produced even more cunning and corrupt offspring, – becoming an elite ruling class. They will devise more sophisticated methods to subjugate and control the masses, in order to minimise the chances of a rebellion. It will become one huge insane asylum, with the mad leading the mad. Mental and physical disease will thrive. The whole thing will spiral out of control. This is life on the astral today, of which earth is a part.

The chances of an individual mind freeing itself from this nightmare depends on how deeply it has submerged its identity in the nonsense of it all. A false notion has been put into circulation that most of what goes on in the world is none of your business. If you accept this, you are effectively controlled by the elite, simply by turning a blind eye and a deaf ear. Every single thing which enters your mind immediately becomes your business. The elite have seen to it that your greatest gift, your mind, lies dormant, cluttered by the thoughts and conflicts, they have planted there and nurtured. Everything in creation is your business. How you use that information is up to you, based on your concept of morality and your

Chapter Six

degree of self-discipline.

Planetary life is submerged in an ocean of problems, because the very vast majority of the population are minding their own business. This situation gives the elite a free hand to do as they please. They are just the planetary servants of their astral masters. This is the origin of the 'satan' concept.

CHAPTER SEVEN

When the mind directs its full attention to a serious enquiry, it begins to store energy, and it's vibrations become finer. The mind, or consciousness, resonates with that which is at the focal point of its attention. Sincere enquiry is the selfless seeking of truth for truth's sake. There is no other consideration. Nothing is ever lost. The mind retains the ability to see into the depths of sensual planetary life and remain at its point of sane balance, without being altered by that which it observes. This is because the mind, which has seen that which is really important, can never forget such an importance.

The mind which has never seen that which is really important, attaches a supposed importance to all kinds of trivial nonsense, such as ideas, opinions, emotions, memories, misconceptions, etc. It becomes bogged down in these trivialities, but it feels 'safe' in this medium level of violence to which it has become accustomed. This 'comfort zone' fits the psyche perfectly, like a soft armchair.

So why should the psyche leave this comfort to venture into the unknown? That's fine, just stay there in the armchair, --if you don't mind spending a thousand more karmic lives filled with nonsense and pain. Why venture into that strange territory where they tell you only mad people go? You see others being dragged from their comfort zones by the torturers, yet you just sit there and wait your turn. Your life and destiny are of the utmost importance, but the life and destiny of others is every bit as important. All are one, temporarily divided by the illusion of separateness, in order to create, establish and maintain the false concept of 'me versus the rest'. Divide and control. The established 'ego' makes the thought-world function. If the egocentric psyche is not maintained, no hidden agenda can be bought to fruition.

Each and every mind has the ability to make life-changing decisions. (*See* Free will). Every moment holds a possible choice to make a conscious decision to change a seemingly unchangeable thought or reaction. Nothing in existence has the power to prevent you from making such a choice. It is the sacred right of every individual, as

Chapter Seven

it is guided by a sacred impulse from the heart of truth. The mind is not just suspended in a field of consciousness. It *is* that consciousness. It has unlimited access to all the knowledge in creation, but has allowed itself to believe otherwise. You don't have to go to some hermit, sitting cross-legged in a cave on a frozen mountain. This is all just pure nonsense, a false trail. Everyone has the same power. If the guru can do it, so can you. (*See* Free will).

The mind which never makes a choice remains a prisoner of the thought-process. You have been taught from birth that thinking is the sole function of the mind. This could not be further from the truth. The power of the mind is infinitely greater than that. It has the free will to either wake to reality or stagnate in the machine. It can begin to look at those thoughts. Thinking you know something and *really* knowing it are not the same thing. Real knowing does not think it knows, it simply knows. There is the silent mind and the thing known. There is no thought in between to distort or colour the thing perceived. Thinking you know something is just the end result of a chain of presumptions, and therefore you only presume you know it. You are merely accepting incoming data as reliable, when in fact, it isn't.

The thought-process is not based on solid ground. If you use a calculator to work out some complex formula, you may get the right answer, but you are only accepting it as correct without knowing why it is right or how the answer was arrived at. On the other hand, the mathematician can work it out without a calculator, and will know exactly how the answer was arrived at. You assume you know the answer, but the mathematician *really* knows. You cannot know anything without understanding it. How do you separate lies from truth? Information is received in two ways, directly and indirectly. All information received directly is known to be true and is transformed into individual knowledge.

Information received indirectly is only assumed to be true but may contain many lies and psychological traps.

A fool with a calculator may get the same answer as a sage without a calculator but the difference is that the fool still knows nothing.

The sage functions in such a way as to make it impossible for a lie to pass through the ultra- alert net of full consciousness, thus maintaining the purity of truth.

The field in which human beings function is an infinitesimal part of an unimaginably vast astral world, in which every conceivable type of thought-entity has its habitation or comfort zone. Everything within the system functions automatically. It is a great fermenting, ever changing mass, where everything is connected directly or indirectly.

In any chain-reaction, the movement of any one link is effected by the movement of any other link, wherever they are in the chain. The fact that the two links are far apart or out of sight makes no difference. They are all governed by that which initiated the original motion. Within the whole there are endless chains, all touching each other, all related. When certain chemicals are mixed there is a reaction. Someone who has studied chemistry knows exactly what the end result will be. There is no freedom in thought. When any process is set in motion, it eventually settles and levels out to form certain characteristics. Look around and see the characteristics of this particular mix, the potholes, the filthy congested cities, the corruption, the lunatic asylums bursting at the seams, filled with minds which could no longer cope with the confusion, etc, etc. The human mind in its present condition is no more than a link in a chain of reactions. This situation can be altered by simply doing the unexpected, that is, acting as opposed to reacting. The machine cannot understand the operator. It can only do what it is programmed to do. It is programmed to react in a particular way to any and every known eventuality, but not the unexpected ones. The only 'spanner in the works' is free action. (*See* Reawakening to Consciousness).

What is thought? When the human mind enters the field of thought, it begins to resonate in tune with that field, the field being the focus of its attention. The mind descends into a stupor, or semi-conscious condition, with just enough awareness to function in the physical world. All thoughts are assumptions based solely on the accumulation of incoming data. Thought knows nothing. Everything is assumed and dumbly accepted. All thought is 'mental noise'. This noise is filled with messages, which are part of an incredibly sophisticated system of codes and symbols. When you look at some amazing new wonder of modern technology, you think 'What a fantastic mind must have put this together!' This is not true. These wonders simply evolved step by step over many years, from the most basic, original ideas, and with much trial and error. Thousands of minds have been involved, each one contributing its penny's worth. These machines are merely the end result of the ever- changing nature of the thought process.

It is exactly the same with these super-sophisticated mind-control devices, evolved over eons. In the thought-machine, every sight, sound, touch and smell holds a message for any mind which happens along. Every aspect of planetary life is speaking to you through the psyche. The psyche is not aware of this as all the messages are subliminal. It is only in a crisis that the mind strives for sincerity. The confused mind looks for answers in the wrong places. It asks the wrong questions because it is out of touch with *real* reality, --because it was deprived of very important knowledge from birth.

CHAPTER EIGHT

Can the mind play tricks on itself? No, it cannot. All trickery and deception only exists in the make-up of the world of thought, and the mind which has identified with it only assumes it can play tricks on, or deceive itself. Many misconceptions have been put into circulation, self-perpetuating lies. One particular notion is that your everyday mind is your 'conscious' mind, and that you can access your 'subconscious' mind, using various mechanical or ritualistic methods. This could not be further from the truth. The exact opposite is true. This lie was designed and put about to misdirect the mind into thinking all is well. If you don't know there is a fault you won't want to fix it. Simple psychology. Just look at it logically. Why should the conscious mind get in touch with the subconscious for answers? It's like the university professor consulting the cleaning-lady on some high-brow scientific theory. The master does not consult the pupil. The pupil consults the master. The fact is that this, your everyday mind is the stupefied, or semi-conscious mind, and in a crisis it can consult your real consciousness, which is usually blotted out by the conflicting nonsense of thought. Your true consciousness really does have all the answers. It is not until you wake from the hypnotic condition that you see the true nature of the 'idiot-soup' they have been spoon feeding you.

Why then, does this all-powerful inner silence not impose itself on the everyday mind to a greater degree? In the first place, the mind, even submerged deeply in the thought process and having become a psyche, still retains the ability to receive these tiny impulses, and either dwell upon them or choose to ignore them. Secondly, there is absolutely no movement in the silence of truth. It is infinitely quiet and delicate. Truth does not 'do' anything. It just is. Would you discuss the finer points of poetry with a rabid Rottweiler? No concept that the human mind could ever conjure up could ever be applied to truth as it really is. You are truth, but you won't know it until you wake from the dream. If truth were to interfere with your free will it would simply cease to be free will, so, *that* can never happen.

The mind or consciousness is constantly receiving sacred energy, the energy which flows through all creation. How the mind chooses to proceed through its life determines how much of this energy is saved or squandered. As this energy enters your mind it is consumed by the aimless jumping about of thoughts which make up mechanical thinking. When the mind decides to make a choice to positively change, some aspect of the mind's direction, energy is stored. This stored energy alters consciousness. When a conscious choice is made to change some seemingly unchangeable thought or reaction, you transform a reaction into action. This resulting action will be a 'conscious action' as opposed to an 'unconscious or automatic reaction'. Thus the world of thought is denied its 'expected reaction' and the automatic cycle is broken.

Reaction is influenced by everything. Action is influenced by nothing. Reaction consumes all available energy. Action consumes no energy. With every further action, more and more energy is stored, further expanding consciousness. Each new choice of action becomes easier, until the mind is fully awake and becomes free of the dream-machine. It is still possible for the mind which has stored energy to lose it all again, if it chooses to return to habitual thinking. The role of the third aspect is to prevent the mind from slipping back into the grey mist of confusion. All reaction is a mechanical process. All action is spontaneous. All reaction is transitory and fleeting. All action is permanent and eternal. When the mind wakes from the reactionary thought-process, it can see with a clarity never even suspected in the world of thought.

As consciousness expands, there are many astonishing discoveries. The waking of consciousness occurs as a series of anti-shocks. This is the undoing or reversal of the hypnotic condition. In the world of thought, all experience takes the form of shocks, or mind-numbing mini- traumas. As the mind withdraws from this process of conditioning, it can feel the effect of great weights being lifted from it. These are the opposite of the concept of physical shocks. The vibrations gradually become finer, leading to a state of ecstatic freedom. Meanwhile, back at the thought-farm! Everyone has free will. The mind which wishes to spend another thousand lifetimes in the karmic world is perfectly free to do so, to offer its service as just another log on the bonfire of human suffering. But the message here is that there is no need to. The false concept of need is just another illusory mechanism. (See Karma).

You will never know about anything if you don't take time out to study it. If you are interested and would like to pursue the above field of enquiry, there arises the obvious question: is it all worth the effort? Yes it is! And that is the biggest understatement in creation. The word 'important' takes on a whole new meaning. The results are infinitely beyond your wildest dreams. Your greatest worldly pleasure is a horrific nightmare by comparison. To say it was like coming out of an eternal night of darkness and pain into a real world of clear fresh air and glorious sunshine, where your heart feels as light as a feather, would be a totally inadequate way of putting it. The mind trapped in the world of thought is living in an atmosphere as thick and black as tar, where the slightest movement is a gargantuan struggle, eating up all your available energy.

CHAPTER NINE

It is almost impossible, but never totally impossible, for the mind, in such a lamentable condition, to even begin to imagine any alternative, let alone the one just described. It is first necessary to look at the sheer stupidity of its present position in a society so corrupt, a rat race where the rats are chasing their own tails. No effort is ever wasted, nothing is lost. Only the nonsense can be dissolved. The real quality of life can never be destroyed. The mind which has shed the nonsense can still enjoy all the good fruits the earth has to offer, only a thousand times more so, and with a new clarity of perception.

The great masses of humanity are crying out from their souls for radical change, but it is the sworn aim of a small number of beings to prevent this at any cost, and maintain the status quo. Hence all the nonsense, the petty trickery, the carefully managed mass hysteria through hypnosis. And what is it all in aid of? To feed the bloodlust of a race of astral monsters, so debased it cannot be imagined. It is a mentality which denies the very existence of truth. It inhabits an illusory limbo, so terrible it cannot be faced, and must be drowned out by total violence and further denial. These creatures of the shadows are spiralling downwards into an ever worsening hell of their own making. Don't let them drag you down with them. It is within your grasp to redirect your mind, find that which is really important, your true identity.

CHAPTER TEN

So what is the overall situation, to sum it all up in a nut shell? There is the ultimate truth, that which is. There is the illusion, that which is not. You find yourself in the illusion. You sense that something is not quite right. You are of a serious frame of mind and would like some answers, but you have not found them. In the meantime, you thrash about in the chaos they keep telling you is life. You go with the flow, but find that it only consists of one crisis after another. You try reading books on the subject. Try this one, it is an attempt to show how it is possible for the mind to find its true identity.

They have confined you to a wheelchair, taught you to wheel yourself about, but what they will never tell you is that you can actually get up and walk. Be careful never to overdo it. If you feel your mind is nearing the edge of some precipice, just pull back and get involved in some mundane activity till things level out, and you feel you can resume where you left off. Remember, the thought-machine will do everything in its power to prevent you from leaving. You will find in-depth explanations in the subject chapters.

A special message to those who would like to study their own minds, but might find the subject a little strange or daunting. Don't worry, there is time to reconsider, before plunging in at the deep end. This is all about ending your suffering, not creating more. Just live your life and try not to harm anyone in any way. Rest assured all will be well. The complicated stuff is just for those who are interested in it and might like to try some of the experiments. The reader may find some of it a trifle 'heavy-going' in places, but will encounter some chapters of particular interest.

Acting

Acting was originally a sacred discipline related to introspection. It developed imagination and visualization. It also helped seeing life from another's point of view. Alas, as it developed and expanded it was hijacked and commercialised, becoming the devil-dance of so-called show business. From there it was further fragmented and used as propaganda disguised as entertainment.

Action and Reaction

The golden rule in all trades which involve cutting to a measurement is 'measure twice and cut once'. The obvious reason is to avoid errors made in haste. If you only measure once a fair percentage of cuts will be wrongly made, involving a costly waste of time, energy and materials. Exactly the same rule applies in everyday situations. Think twice and act once. In most situations individuals think only once or not at all. The result is a society of chaos where everybody reacts automatically. Action is never automatic. Reaction is always automatic. The result can be a catastrophe which could have been avoided. It goes much deeper than that though. (*See* Reawakening to Consciousness.)

Every time you react you become a component in a thought machine which was created by monsters. That's how sinister it is. (*See* Demons and Human Suffering.)

The machine says you need a reason for everything you do. These are not your own reasons, but the machine's reasons. There is no such thing as a free reason. A reason is no more than a trigger for a mechanical response. True action is the manifestation of the spirit in the physical world. It is a purely spontaneous and totally free spiritual impulse. If you need a reason to do something you are a slave to the pre-set code of some authority. (*See* Authority.)

Try to see beyond the reason and do what you think is right, rather than expedient. What is ten minutes if it saves a life or lives? Remember you are a human being and not a slave to some non-human agenda. (*See* Humanity.)

Within the parameters of thought only reaction is possible. The free mind does not need to explain itself or report to any authority. That is the essence of a sacred impulse. (*See* Impulses.)

The mind functions on sacred impulses but the psyche functions on mechanical urges. Although the psyche receives sacred impulses these are largely drowned out by the noise of conflicting thoughts. The psyche is particularly subject to emotions which give rise to hasty reactions. If you hate, you become part of the very thing you hate by adding another flame to the inferno. If you surround yourself with a cool sea of calmness it not only forms a firebreak but quenches the flames it touches.

Alertness

Without the quality of alertness the mind has no safeguard against encroaching thoughts. Alertness is literally the guardian of the mind. It functions at a far greater speed than the cleverest thought and cannot be outwitted by it. It is always one step ahead. It is *Superthought*. It is instantly aware. It is unknown to the psyche as it is a timeless quality existing beyond time. It can be aware of and concentrate on many aspects simultaneously. It sees the whole picture of the finished jigsaw where the psyche has to crawl laboriously from piece to piece. (*See* Reawakening to Consciousness.)

Arrogance

Arrogance manifests in two forms. There is the morbid arrogance of the non-human psyche which sees itself as superior to humanity. There is the pseudo-arrogance of the human psyche which springs from the fear of vulnerability due to many inner conflicts and complexes.

Art

Art is that which bypasses everyday conditioning and touches the sensitivity of the real inner being. It shines a light into the darkest corners. There are many art forms. Much of what poses as art today is a joke, merely causing observers to scratch their heads.

Attention

All you see is all you have, all there is. There is no such thing as the future. It simply does not exist. This fact cannot be stressed too much. You must think deeply about this to see the truth of it. The concept of future is a hook on which demons hang their false promises. There is only a changing now. This is why so-called time travel is possible. It is all here and now and under the proper conditions it is all accessible to consciousness.

The concept of future effectively robs the present of full consideration. All action takes place now, not in some wishy-washy wonderland they call future. In reality, future means never. The concept of future is simply a device whereby truth may be poked indefinitely into the long grass. All promises are equally worthless. There is not a single process which cannot begin right now this very moment and with immediate effect, thus eliminating the need for the concept of a promise. Such action in the real active now would render its fruition a real possibility by bringing the new concept within the framework of, and under the spotlight of full consideration.

Those wishing to kill off any new concept talk about a wonderful future, thus keeping everyone a prisoner in the psychological straightjacket of the impotent condition of hope. Is it not logical that after hundreds of years of promises you should by now have arrived at something resembling that promised wonderland? Is it not strange that you have not? Is this not the future they talked about then?

Is it not patently obvious that any process which has already begun needs not even the shadow of a promise? No need to hope folks, it's here now. Beginning a process tomorrow means 'sorry not today'. Can you detect the scent of a rodent on the evening breeze? Just imagine a world without promises. The choice is yours, now or never.

Now is a choice. It can be an action. It can be a reaction. It is up to you.

You have free will, the ability to change yourself and the world around you. Do not ask about an imaginary past or future. Look at now, find out what is wrong with it and put it right as best you can. They are introducing beliefs, concepts and labels into this now. They tell you this is Sunday, the sun goes down, the sun comes up, they tell you this is Monday and you believe them.

Go to a point on the planet where the sun does not go down and look for tomorrow. Every aspect of your life is governed by these beliefs, concepts and labels. Your attention is being fragmented. The whole of your attention is being departmentalised into points of focus on the false concepts of past and future. Now does not create the future. Now creates now. The false concept of future diverts your attention from now into an imaginary hinterland which gives rise to emotions such as anxiety, dread, hope and worry.

The changed aspect of now which your memory regards as an imagined past gives rise to emotions such as anger, annoyance, bias, guilt, frustration, fury, hatred, paranoia, regret, revenge, resentment, spite and suspicion. Your attention in the spontaneous living now, the reality in the present moment, is non-existent. This is because your attention is contaminated and distorted by emotions attached to memories.

Only sacred impulses exist in the now. Because your attention is so crowded by these emotions and the psyche is in a condition of inner confusion and conflict you are blind to the finer sensitivities of now. You are just struggling on in the condition of morbid servitude to the will of unseen and unsuspected influences. All this unnecessary nonsense destroys the happiness of the moment. (*See* Kundalini.)

Authority

Authority says one must obey the will of another. One fool dances to the tune of another fool. The average psyche accepts as deadly serious what is nothing more than the whims of perverted popinjays backed up by their club-wielding, knuckle-dragging vassals. You go through hell and high water to prop up a status quo which dictates you should lie dying in twelve inches of mud with phosphorous in your lungs and white hot shrapnel in your guts, knowing you are dying to preserve a way of living where back home the privileged sneering perverts vomit over each other in palaces of stolen pink marble and violate your women and children as your body sinks in the mud.

You lie there like a jelly-fish, not knowing what bits are still attached. Your awareness wavers on the edge as it hears your last wheeze calling you a hero. A peaceful smile plays across your twitching lips. The satisfaction of a job well done. The rest of your face looks back at you from a tree. You are too far gone now to notice your right arm waving to you from what used to be a hawthorn bush. It's only a week before Christmas but that upside down jeep is not decorated with fairy lights, – they're your toes. Those objects bouncing off your shattered skull are not coconuts either. Your awareness drifts back to a balmy evening in your memory bank and you finally lose touch with that wriggling piece of tenderised meat which was the fool in the mud.

Authority has no respect whatsoever for those foolish enough to obey its dictates. Never obey the orders of another. Reclaim your life before it is too late. By obeying orders you are surrendering your freedom. The concept of authority is no more than a trick in a fool's playground. It is the mother and father of all bluffs. Authority by its very nature can only function through secrecy. If all knowledge was shared there could be no authority. The demons and their popinjays only exist because you lack the real courage to disobey and give peer pressure the two-fingered salute. So much for authority.

Avoiding Radical Solutions

Reality is totally simple. Humanity has been dragged from its simple happy roots for so long its true origin now seems like a fictitious fable. It has been conditioned to believe that facts and figures can express truth. You can plough through all the facts and figures in creation and all you'll find is the lunacy of the world you live in. Each volume shows more of the same problems without offering a radical solution. There are no solutions in literature which concerns itself with the physical world alone, as this is merely an extension of the astral, and in turn the spiritual realms. These books examine only one piece of the jig-saw without even being aware of all the other pieces. The authors of such volumes are not to blame as the vast majority are sincere in their efforts to expose the engineered injustices which have turned society into a travesty. It's like listening to the constant drip from a leaky roof. The solution to any problem or unsatisfactory situation must be radical. It is a case of all or nothing. By becoming involved with facts and figures you are losing touch with your original simplicity.

Instead of listening to the drips go and fix the leak. You'll soon forget the drips. Don't tell yourself you'll do it. You don't need the permission of your ego to do what your higher being tells you must be done. Then you have a radical action which transforms your life and the lives you touch. To do this you must go beyond the physical to the real causes of the supposedly accidental chaos on earth. This leads to the think tanks in the world of thought where all subhuman plots are hatched. Go straight for the jugular and expose those vicious cowards who hide in the shadows of the greater world of thought and operate in the physical world through their perverted lackeys.

Belief

To begin with there is only the unknown. With regard to any question, you either know the answer or you don't. If you do not know, it is essential that you honestly accept the fact, thus leaving open the possibility that at some juncture you may investigate it more deeply, perhaps arrive at a logical conclusion. Such a conclusion would resolve the question, while dissolving it on a permanent basis. Through the medium of logic a question can be answered. Once a question is answered through logic the question itself ceases to exist, thus reducing the level of clutter in the psyche. (*See* logic.)

On the other hand, if you blindly accept somebody else's answer to a question without investigating it for yourself, the ghost of the question remains like an unfinished symphony of loose ends, cluttering up the psyche. To blindly believe anything is to create a condition in which your life is being effectively controlled by others.

The stage hypnotist carefully picks out subjects before putting them through their paces. Using a quick-fire method of suggestion, these individuals can be made to do anything, believe anything. What is taking place on stage is not as isolated as the audience thinks. They leave the theatre totally unaware that what they have just witnessed is but a small example of the mental trickery they are subjected to, every day of their lives, and have come to accept as normal everyday living.

The population is controlled in two ways; through open lies, and through subliminal activity. To begin with, they (the population), can do nothing about the subliminal stuff, simply because they are as yet unaware of its existence. This is why subliminal control is so effective. If they begin to question every situation and see through the open lies, they will clear away enough of the mist of confusion to expose the bottomless pit of deception which brings utter chaos to their beautiful planet, and its beautiful inhabitants. The shock of realization will trigger a new awareness of the convert, subliminal activity. Once detected, the lie ceases to be effective. The same with the subliminal stuff, which will evaporate likewise. Only then will they know the true nature of blind belief in false concepts, which have kept their minds asleep. The psyche is your sleeping mind, or lowered consciousness. You are what you eat, both physically and mentally. Without proper nutrition the body quickly deteriorates. The same applies to the psyche. (*See* Psyche.)

If the psyche isn't fed with truths it will have nothing but false concepts to work with. This throws it into a condition of torpor, caused by confusion. It descends into a habitual stumbling, from day to day, a life deprived of all meaning and purpose, a life of clichéd stultification. There is no difference between this condition and that of a herd of cattle in a field, moving automatically from patch to patch of fresh grass, totally oblivious to the farmer's plan for them; the way they are bred, bought and sold, milked and brutally murdered in their prime of life. The cow's life of servitude is rewarded with a baptism of terror, making a mockery of all those days spent in green meadowland, listening to birdsong, trusting implicitly in their mysterious masters.

Comes the final day of the animal's life; finds itself forced into a truck crammed with its fellow beings, all aboard for an uncomfortable trip to the site of execution. It isn't the death itself that is so terrible, but what leads up to it. The actual death is one merciful release. They are forced into a large fenced-in area, already swarming with their own kind. Next thing, several monsters are moving in, wielding heavy clubs, thus causing horrific pain as well as trauma and forcing the poor beasts forward. The onslaught proceeds without respite, until the next truck pulls in. What a betrayal by the trusted masters who tuned out to be such monsters. The confused mass surges towards the narrowing fences at the far end of the enclosure. An infectious nausea spreads through the trapped herd as they hear the cries of the beaten ones and smell the hot blood wafting back from somewhere beyond. They lose control of their bodily functions slipping and falling in their own excrement. They are forced through the narrowing fences towards the stench of death. Their eyes bulge with terror and they try to escape by climbing over the fences but slip back in eight inches of excrement. The cow's psyche is in turmoil. A vague awareness of something mysteriously imminent plays round the edges of the all-consuming terror. Now the fences are too close together to attempt escape and those in front are forced into single file as they near the hole in the wall of the great edifice of the unknown.

The smell of the hot blood is overpowering. The few at the front are now drained of all resistance and stumble forward, numb with terror. The barrier at the hole slides back to admit the next victim, then slides shut again to prevent the next one following. There is a loud crack and the one in the hole falls to the floor in a lifeless heap of marketable beef which is saturated by these last vibrations of terror.

As soon as the limbs cease kicking from the nervous reaction a chain is fixed around a hind leg and the stolen body is hoisted to the bloodbath on the next floor. This floor resembles a swimming pool, with four inches of blood lapping at its sides. The carcass is slit open and the steaming blood splashes into waiting churns. Now it is your turn. The barrier slips back and you are pushed into the clamour and stench of the slaughterhouse. A monster steps forward and fires a heavy bolt into your skull. Before your body falls, the bolt, which is attached to a cable is quickly withdrawn from what was your skull and reloaded ready for the next shot. Your astral thought-form drifts away, taking with it all its beliefs in readiness for its next karmic experience. (*See* karma.)

The murder machine clicks up another digit and within the hour the terrified cow's earthly body is processed, boned and packed ready for consumption. With all your dreams and aspirations you stand no more chance than the cattle if you go on lying in the meadow, blindly believing. There is always something buried deep within your psyche which tells you to question things but you mostly ignore it. Do your own thinking. Don't let others do it for you. Always listen, but never believe. Many questions await your attention. Do you drift through your life accepting everything as ordained? Do you look at life and wonder why?

Boredom

The morbid psyche is vaguely aware of being hemmed in by its condition and is at a loss to know the why and wherefore of its existence. This is compounded by the establishment which methodically starves it of any meaningful education. Being left to its own devices and in the dark, it craves meaning in the emptiness. It is provided with no alternatives to temporal games and entertainment. All these activities are organised to occupy the psyche. It deflects the attention away from the prevailing sense of loss of a real way of living.

Once the psyche pursues self-indulgence it becomes automatically caught up in a pendulum mode where its whole life consists of highs and lows. The low points can manifest as a depression or the less severe condition of boredom. These negative conditions would not exist if instead of highs and lows the psyche pursued a natural constant level process of living resulting from a true education. Such a way of life would be full of interest and excitement with a sense of completeness and fulfilment.

Cogitation and Thought

Cogitation is the true free-flowing function of a clear human mind, its very essence. It is the sole property of a mind and cannot be influenced by any external entity. This is why the phenomenon of thought was introduced as a 'foot in the door' by a predatory entity on the astral or mental level.

Thought is introduced into a clear mind in order to distract pure cogitation and set up an apparent alternative backed up by the cunning use of language. This phenomenon is the first seed of temptation, the first knock on the door, the intake of breath before the scream, the missionary before the soldiers, the shadow of the falling sledge-hammer.

The whole world of thought is a fully automatic process, a cybernetic self-perpetuating machine. Physical language is a backup system of labels supposed to convey particular meanings for thoughts. Communication in the world of thought demands the use of language.

So how does cogitation differ from thought? How important is this question? This question is of the utmost importance as it takes you to the very heart of planetary chaos and human suffering. It is the most relevant question in the world today.

Cogitation is seeing the actuality of a situation. Thought can see nothing. The reason why cogitation can see with absolute clarity is because of the total absence of thought, the absence of deception and self-deception.

Thought, by its very nature is unstable as it is a fragmented phenomenon made up of individual thoughts, the essence of which have no foundation in reality and are in constant flux. Thoughts do not even have stability in their own illusory world. All thought is based on supposition. All supposition is heavily biased. So thought can see nothing as it actually is in reality. There is always a bias, causing distortion.

No entity can deceive or control through the medium of cogitation as its evil intent would be instantly exposed. Unless you strive for absolute truth all you are left with is useless theories which you spend the rest of your life trying to justify so as not to look too stupid in the eyes of your peers.

The experiment with a matchbox in the chapter on Images, Labels and Words offers a glimpse of the difference between 'thinking you see' and 'seeing without thought.'

Compassion

Compassion is when you feel someone else's pain more than your own, when you are genuinely more concerned about the well-being of others than about your own. Is it not logical that if everyone on earth felt that way life on earth would be a paradise? The sum total of any society is the interaction between its inhabitants. Psyches are geared to work against each other, thus ensuring division and conquest. All human beings have compassion but when a non-human influence is introduced it causes chaos. The non-human has no compassion and therefore is incapable of interacting with human beings in a natural way.

A clear human mind can never be fragmented. This fragmentation has created societies based solely on bluff, bluster, greed and cunning. In such a society the human psyche is defenceless against the non-human psyche.

Competition

They tell you competition is all about winning and you believe them. This is a classic example of misdirection. The truth is that competition is all about losing. For every winner there are thousands of losers. That is from the perspective of sport and gambling.

From the perspective of politics and finance, competition begins as an apparently fair system but eventually transforms itself into a totalitarian monopoly where criminals dispense bribes and fix prices as the strong devour the weak.

The above state of affairs is not in any way a natural progression but is forced on the population by stealth. In real terms the concept of competition is the introduction of struggle, infighting and false hopes into the human psyche.

Conspiracies

Do you think for one moment that those unscrupulous individuals who seized material riches and power in the past could ever give up this power? If you do you are a very long way from being streetwise. Belief in such a scenario is the very essence of naivety. Any society which functions on a monetary system as opposed to a humanitarian system is by its very nature conspiratorial.

You look around and try to make sense of what you see. You dive under the surface to seek the hidden causes. You think you see the causes but the real causes go much deeper than the ones you see.

This is because the actual original causes go far deeper than you think. These creatures thrive on doublethink. The real nature of the games they play make top-level chess look like tiddlywinks. So you keep digging till you finally catch up with the careering route-ends of the ultimate conspiracy.

Conspiracies do not just go away. They become ever more manipulative as more and more individuals are insidiously drawn into its periphery. This ensures its perpetuity, rotting society to the core. It becomes impossible to stop. One thing is absolutely certain, it will never ever stop itself. By its very nature a conspiracy will deny its own machinations. So don't believe anyone who tries to tell you there are no conspiracies. They are either a naive fool or part of the very conspiracy they are denying. The only reason conspiracies are thriving is because you have allowed yourself to be led to believe they do not exist. Wake up.

Control

(Conditioning, manipulation and control of the human psyche)

The influences that control humanity employ many methods. These fall into five main categories:

1—The open encouragement of trivial activities, such as sports, contests, money-lotteries, newspapers, books, plays and films with propagandist content, mild eroticism, nonsense cultures aimed at vulnerable children, in order to drive a wedge between young and old, thus establishing a destructive 'generation gap'. The aim of this category is to divert the human psyche as far as possible from matters which seriously affect its freedom and real quality of life.

2 —Turning a blind eye to harmful, anti-social activities, allowing them to thrive, while pretending to oppose them. These activities include the drug culture, paedophilia, negative sexual activities ranging from rape to so-called 'snuff movies', crime and corruption in general. The aim of this category is to spread corruption, strife and fear through humanity, thus rotting society from the inside.

3—Sophisticated 'double-think' or psychological misdirection. This includes the circulation of self-perpetuating lies, selective facts, propaganda heavily disguised as news media items, supposedly open discussion, --the real purpose of which is to debunk any attempt to make the real. Truth known, lies woven into the indoctrination of children and labelled 'education', the perpetuation of atrocities and pointing the finger elsewhere, secret think-tanks, the purpose of which is to constantly review and update all of the above psychological trickery. These think-tanks are composed of unbelievably devious individuals who delight in and live only for their role among the hierarchy. The aim of this category is to allay any suspicions and throw the human psyche off guard.

4—Covert criminal activity by so-called elected governments, such as genetic engineering involving food, humans and animals, blackmail, hypnosis and mind control, torture and murder, extermination programmes through artificially-created wars, laboratory-created diseases and the destruction of food crops. The aim of this category is to exterminate unwanted populations and keep territories in the iron grip of planted dictators.

5—The use of so-called 'black magic' – a real force in the physical world. This is the ultimate abuse and perversion of esoteric knowledge. This highly secret activity is used to control events through the psyches of selected individuals in positions of influence, who otherwise might become 'loose cannons'. The aim of this category is to ensure ultimate planetary control from the very top. The one great fear of the controllers of earth is the real magic of truth.

Some examples of long term agendas:-- If someone hides a pebble under a mountain of pebbles, you cannot prove it. That's the beauty of secrecy. But an intelligent mind does not need proof. The very concept of proof is false. Supposed proof is no more than a ploy to maintain the blind- belief system, and to ensure the impotence of the believing psyche, -- an accepted formula to bolster the original belief, just because someone said so, a prescribed formula to effectively stop any further inquiry.

Intelligence sees the whole picture and knows exactly what is taking place. Secrecy is necessary to control any individual or population against their will. The whole culture of secrecy develops from there.

The aim of any dictatorship is to subjugate the population to the point where rebellion is impossible. There can be no half measures. The suppressors of truth know full well they are as good as finished, if they release their grip of iron, even for a moment, as life becomes a nonsensical hell for all but the chosen ones who grovel to the elite few. The corruption seeps down through societies, taking many forms and touching every life in a negative way. Many are drawn into the periphery of the core of evil. This is how it really is, and not just an accidental mess, as they would have you believe. Just look around. One of their aims is to destroy the social cohesion and community spirit of the population. High rise housing was one method of achieving this. By demolishing perfectly good streets of houses and herding the people into tower blocks, it left the streets in the trustworthy hands of thugs and junkies. It created a wasteland, with families stacked vertically, like caged animals in a pet shop. It needed only one generation of this to destroy a community that took many generations to build. Even if all high-rises were demolished now, the damage is done. Mission accomplished.

Another example of social engineering – Old established populations are pushed out of their neighbourhoods by stealth through rising rents. This is done to clear the areas for fat cats to move in where they are convenient to city centres. These areas are cleaned up for the wealthy while the original rightful inhabitants are socially fragmented and forced to try their luck in badly built boxes in out of the way open air prisons they call 'estates'.

Public services have distanced their management from the public, so as to render complaints ineffectual. Arrogant individuals, surreptitiously installed in positions of power, make inexplicable decisions in direct opposition to the will of the people. These are the tentacles of the elite, and answerable to no one. A deliberate policy of mass-immigration, on the flimsiest of pretexts, is designed to create a cheap labour market, while destroying the hard-won rights of local workers. Every country has a secret establishment which always remains in control no matter which political party is elected. All politics is a confidence trick, and all politicians are cardboard cut-outs, dangling like puppets.

The reason why certain individuals can order the indiscriminate massacre of innocents is because they have no empathy with human beings. They have no empathy because they are non- humans, detesting every human aspiration. They are either direct descendants of the original deniers of truth or hybrids of themselves engineered to do their dirty work. These creatures see the results of these atrocities as positive in the following ways.

1 – They create chaos and tit-for-tat violence by pointing the finger elsewhere.
2 – They reduce populations.
3 – They serve particular political agendas.
4 – They produce mass suffering.
5 – The resulting mass migration supplies cheap labour for other countries.

Mass immigration dilutes the cultural cohesion of the indigenous population. It weakens its resilience and ability to fight back against the jackboot of an oppressive regime. It supplies greedy employers with cheap labour, further weakening local workers by starving them of dignity, money and hope. It causes strife and infighting among the ever diversified-population. This creates the perfect excuse for evermore brutal policing policies.

The new immigrants couldn't care less as they are too happy to lick the backsides of their new bosses.

The creation of false monetary break downs are labelled 'economic recessions', to bring the population further to its knees. Economic booms are created whenever large scale reconstruction or modernisation is desired. The latest ploy to tighten their grip on humanity operates through falsely- created concepts such as 'political correctness', human rights and health and safety regulations. Once these concepts have been accepted by the docile population, new laws are created with the ultimate aim of gagging free speech. It encourages people to spy on each other and create an atmosphere of mistrust and fear, a witch hunt in which anybody can be victimised by the establishment. A crooked legal system with built-in loop holes, gives rights to the criminals, releases paedophiles into the public domain and takes away the rights of innocent people by criminalizing them over nonsensical trivialities. Falsely created panic and fear of circulated diseases gives credence to the injection of children with dubious substances, under the guise of 'immunization'.

Every other day (and night), jet aircraft and drones disperse harmful chemicals into the atmosphere, over towns and cities mainly, causing mental and physical illnesses. An ever increasing number of radio masts seriously affect human brain waves. A great many individuals can detect an electronic hum or buzz which they are led to believe is the condition of tinnitus. There are satellites, of unknown purpose –how many of them encircling the planet at all times? There's also genetic engineering, involving humans, animals and food. Police forces are issued with guns, rubber bullets and tasers, to subdue public gatherings, in preparation for large-scale protests at the abuse of power. There are experimental gases, lasers and sonics. The list goes on forever.

They have sonics which can bring you to your knees with a splitting headache and lasers which cause temporary or permanent damage to your eyesight.

Lotteries do absolutely nothing for the welfare of the people. One obscenely large pay out of, say, thirty or forty million, as against many laughably small pay outs, merely rewards a few members of the working masses, leaving the remainder to try their luck again. If, instead, they paid out five thousand prizes of, say, ten thousand each, then society would really benefit, and the odds of winning would be greatly increased. The public is being hoodwinked by the present system, which amounts to nothing more than an involuntary tax.

A news media, (so-called), radio, the press, television, is either owned or controlled by the vassals of the elite. Edited news items consist of lies and selected truths, rigged interviews and talk shows, phone-ins, --where any hint of conspiracy is immediately laughed off the airwaves. The media generates a constant flow of trivial, contrived controversy, mental trash, to occupy the public psyche while they are being led on, stealthily, like lambs to the slaughter.

The media constantly mouth false concepts such as 'our political masters' when the very same politicians were originally elected to be 'our political servants', serving only the will of the people.

Any government has and always have had the ability to stamp out the drug culture, permanently and with immediate effect. But the establishment will never allow it. The drug culture is a wonderful way to stupefy youth, to maintain inner conflict and fragmentation of societies, as is crime in general. Excessive use of alcohol or so-called recreational drugs drive the psyche imperceptibly down into a spiral to total slavery. There is only one solution. Stop taking alcohol and drugs to excess immediately. Just remember there is no tomorrow. Now is filled with magic. Just open the door and go there. You will find that magic. It's your only chance. Ghastly noise, purporting to be music, has been foisted on the public by stealth. Violent rhythms, primal beats with anti-social messages of harm and mayhem, infest this infernal racket, glorifying drugs, casual sex and infidelity, is foisted subliminally on the psyches of impressionable children, in the form of words recorded in reverse, anagrams and words speeded up or slowed down to evade cursory notice. Real talent is largely ignored, or even suppressed, as it would have a positive effect on the psyche. Identity cards are on the way in, --just another cunning ploy to reduce all to 'serf' status. You can forget all about that 'John Citizen' tag!

Humanity's birthright was to live independently and freely on the land of its birth, build its own dwellings, grow its own food, develop its own skills and live in harmony with itself and its surroundings. However, human beings were tricked by the caretakers, removed by stealth from the land and forced to settle in cesspits of corruption they called cities, once in these cesspits they were thereafter trapped as slaves to a money system, the ultimate aim of which will be the ability to rule the whole planet and destroy any life at the touch of a red button.

In numerology W = 6. The internet, aptly named the 'world wide web' (WWW = 666). Many millions of human children fly into the web where the funnel-web spiders devour them unseen in the shadows.

There is the ever increasing use of initials in place of plain talking. This keeps the casual listener or reader at arm's length.

Whenever they are challenged in the event of their corrupt activity being exposed they come out with a smattering of prepared condescending platitudes such as 'rogue elements', 'errors of judgement', 'misguided enthusiasm', 'there have been administrative errors', 'we've been working with false analysis', 'there have been missed opportunities', 'lessons have been learned', 'reforms are in place', 'it will never happen again', 'it's time we moved on' and 'that's an end of the matter'. The above gobbledegook is composed in such a way as to avoid legal challenge.

Certain words have become repugnant to the public psyche. These words are substituted by less offensive alternatives, for example; instead of saying 'privatised' they now use the word 'outsourced'.

When a scandal of epic proportions threatens the lifestyles of the establishment protective mechanisms automatically react. Some individual crawls out of the woodwork and assumes the mantle of 'man of the people', 'righter of wrongs'. 'I'll sort this lot out, see if I don't.' (Usually a journalist, radio presenter or politician). These individuals are usually very fast talkers with a cunning intellect.

How to spot the fake. A genuine individual will be quickly silenced.

An insincere individual will be easily manipulated by members of the establishment with something to hide.

The fake will never ask (or permit to be asked) the very questions which really need to be asked. They use methods such as, 'we've run out of time, we'll have to leave it there.'

The fake (in a live discussion) will suddenly and rudely interrupt to change the subject.

The fake will constantly interject with irrelevancies to dilute the seriousness of the debate.

The fake (in radio phone-ins) will interject with, 'traffic reports, news bulletins, or the line will be 'bad'. Suddenly the line will be cut off deliberately if there is the slightest hint of anything damaging to the establishment being said. 'Oops, we seem to have lost that caller, we'll try to get you back.' But they never do. The fake will devote most of a so-called phone-in to hosting heavily biased 'experts'. They spill over each other in a torrent of obsequious acquiescence. As the 'expert' smugly shoots the official line in an insipid monotonous drone.

The fake leads the listeners to believe they have someone who really cares to speak out for them, but little do they suspect that ultimately their hopes will be dashed as the fake slowly kills off the inquiry.

The purpose of these individuals, who are pawns of the establishment is to play for time till some other rabbit can be pulled from the hat of public perception.

There are many such individuals waiting in the wings. There's one to suit every emergency. They spring out of the woodwork as required to give false hope to a bewildered public at any point in a political process, a succession of fake life lines to justice. This is to forestall public protests.

They hijacked the media long ago and now use that media to conceal the appropriate dots. This is why the gullible public never join the dots, because they are so well hidden. Job done.

As for the millions who sense the injustice of it all, the liars do after-all have the police, the army and their laws. So there.

Lying is a matter of policy. It makes no difference when the lie is found out. The liars are well aware of the profound impact of first impressions on the public psyche. Job done.

Look at the sudden 'apparently incidental' surge in planetary chaos. To what degree is it orchestrated?

Events have been manipulated by stealth. The ultimate weapon of the controllers has been the concept of sleepers. These are clandestine groups, couples and individuals planted in every society world-wide. Because of their deceptive chameleonic nature they had no trouble worming their way into human society. They are also consummate actors, infiltrating every group, primed and ready to jump on any bandwagon and steer it to suit a particular agenda, while feeding back inside information to the controllers.

Once rooted, they help others of the same ilk into positions of influence, thus secretly increasing their numbers. These sleepers are now being activated everywhere in a final push for the complete enslavement of humanity.

Just as they have planted triggers in the deep levels of your psyche they have planted sleepers as triggers in the very heart of your societies.

Shifting Focus

Everybody knows about the concept of insider dealing but nothing can stop it because of the many layers of secrecy involved. The corrupt proceeds of such activities are hidden away in a network of secret banking systems.

The greater scandal is drowned by pushing it beneath the waves of a lesser scandal, or if there isn't a suitable lesser scandal, some concocted controversy. This kills off the original impact of the greater scandal. The trick is in the timing. Job done.

When workers go on strike they are accused of 'holding the public to ransom.' In fact the very same workers are themselves the 'public', and it is the establishment who are holding the public to ransom by victimising one section of the public at a time while referring to the remainder as the 'public'. Job done.

Cutting the wage bill. Step one. Talk about shutting down a business which will destroy the lives of thousands of workers, making their miserable lives even more miserable. Step two. Allow those workers to stew till their psyches are parboiled by worry. Step three. Suddenly come up with the magical solution. The slaves will be so relieved that they will carry on slaving for even lower wages than before. Job done.

The so-called middle classes (with their white collars and penny pay rises) have been specially bred and conditioned to protect the useless elite perverts from the fury of the workers. Where the conditioning fails, bribery, coercion and blackmail are used. Job done.

One of the ploys used to protect paedophiles and cloak their activities goes as follows. In the event of a huge public outcry over the activities of those creatures in high places. Step one. Spread false rumours about a completely innocent individual. One of the functions of sleepers is to start such false rumours. So that's no problem. Step two. Allow the public psyche to be fed the idea of the individual's guilt. The old trick 'no smoke without fire' never fails. The victim screams about such terrible treatment and the politicians immediately jump on the band wagon. 'Look what you've put this lovely saintly individual through. This must never happen again.' They then proceed to threaten a severe punishment for anyone who dares to point a finger at those in high places ever again. The sleepers agree, and so does the stupefied public. Job done.

Every referendum is preceded by a bag of tricks in order to force public opinion in a particular direction. Step one. Speeches containing subliminal threats. Step two. As the need arises the threats become more obvious. Step three. If the public still resists as the vote draws near some major incident occurs, often costing innocent lives. The shock waves have the desired effect. Job done. However, if the masses still somehow manage to vote 'the wrong way' the full fury of the enraged establishment will be unleashed in the form of an insanely vicious collective punishment. A punishment by any other name is still a punishment.

Playing for time – the relentless saturation of the public psyche through their media by an issue of great concern till the public become 'sick to death' of hearing about it. The issue is then quietly brushed under the carpet while the same old system ticks away unnoticed in the background. Job done.

In order to mask the depth of their cunning and to dull the scent of conspiracy, the establishment have planted stooges among the ranks of the masses, who's task it is to constantly label them stupid. Thus effectively removing the conspiratorial element from their decisions in the same way that murderers plead not guilty by reason of insanity.

The members of governments bathe in the full glare of the spotlight of public awareness and take all the flak while the real puppet masters hide in the shadows behind the secret think tanks.

The invisible hand works through the domino effect, the most innocuous incident may be part of a chain of events leading to the eventual fulfilment of any desired agenda while the original incident will never be connected in hindsight. Hence no evidence of orchestration. Job done.

The Pyramid of Psychological Control

Within the pyramid, each level has control over all levels below and is answerable to the level above. Within each level there may be any number of lesser pyramids of control. At the very apex are a hand-picked few from a particular thought-entity, blood group or family.

On level two are a selection of the most trusted members of the group, holding their positions under pain of death.

On level three are the remaining group members holding their positions under pain of death.

On level four are hand-picked outsiders holding their positions under pain of death.

Below this level there is no knowledge of or connection with the controlling blood group. They only know of the level immediately above.

On level five are a large number of outsiders holding their positions under pain of death. Level six works for level five. Level seven works for level six. Level eight works for level seven and so on to the billions who slave their miserable lives away in total ignorance, their only release being death.

Every pyramid of control has but one single head. Each level acts as a cushion to protect the one above from the levels below. Each cushion manifests in the form of a committee or board of directors who show a public face in the same way that politicians take the flak for the shadowy figures of the establishment. This is *why* you will never know the true identity of those who control every aspect of your life.

To you, life is a confused painful mess. To *them*, it's an amusing game.

Creation and Free Will

The popular view of life on earth is of a solid material world in which you find yourself with a mentality which senses that world. You were probably told there is a god up there somewhere beyond the sky watching your every move. So you go through life blindly accepting what your elders tell you. They tell you to be god-fearing. Have you ever known a really good, loving, all-forgiving person? Did you fear that person? Assuming the god of your imagination is infinitely more loving and forgiving than any mortal, there should be no reason to fear such a god. What could such a wonderful god possibly do to make you afraid? (*See* God)

The Illusion of All Possibilities and the Concept of Time

All the knowable environment is the product of an imagination which can create any thing or concept. Very little of it is the product of your imagination, but of one which created the concept of time, space, motion and thought itself. You are a part of that all-knowingness but within the illusion of time you have lost that vital connection. It is now up to you alone to study and come to understand the nature of the illusion and reawaken to your true identity as part of that all-knowing imagination. When you dream at night everything seems real and perfect in every detail but when you wake up you realise it was virtual reality. When people talk about a beginning they are following a false trail. The concepts of beginning and ending are just aspects of this virtual reality.

There is that which exists. There is that which appears to exist but does not. That which does not exist denies that which exists and that denial maintains the illusion. That which exists is unknowable as it is beyond the concept of knowledge which is an aspect of non-existence. The ultimate reality cannot be known but can be seen by an intelligence which has transcended the concept of knowledge and the apparent reality of non-existence. All concepts of knowledge end with the dawning of full consciousness. It is a matter of seeing, not knowing as all knowledge is an illusion.

There is the pull between existence and non-existence which remains invisible to the spark of awareness which is in denial. The free will only sees what it is willing itself to see. The individual free will has the potential ability to create all possibilities, as non-existence is a blank sheet for the individual creator. An intelligence which has transcended thought but has not yet seen reality directly can still feel the pull of existence. If it strives for the truth behind everything it is not in denial and has the ability to find the truth it seeks. If it chooses to ignore the pull it remains in denial and quickly slips back into the illusion.

The unfolding or experiencing of the creation of all possibilities gives rise to the illusion of time, space, motion and thought. The reader is not concerned with the exploration of the never-ending possibilities of non-existence, just this planetary journey through the physical and mental aspects of the local illusion. The objective is to be free of it, not become more deeply immersed in it. To be free of it does not mean to leave it altogether, but to observe all its aspects while the observing mind remains uninfluenced by that which it observes.

There are only two types of psyche in the illusion. You are in denial or you are seeking truth. There are no shades of grey. You are part of the machine or you are not. Each spark of awareness is making its way from non-existence to existence, a particle of dust drifting through a sunbeam on its way to settle somewhere. Those who do not strive for truth further the fragmentation process and create for themselves an even more complex illusion. You look around and think about everything you see and think you know. Whether it is real and solid remains to be investigated. At this starting point you know almost nothing but have the gift of logical deduction to work with. You do know that all this seemingly solid matter has to originate somewhere somehow. This implies a point where it does not exist. Logic is undeniable and lets you know that all that matter has to originate from a state of nothingness and not just be mutated from another phenomenon, as the question would then still remain as to the origin of the other phenomenon. All phenomena mutated or not, fall within the concept of the material illusion.

Logic lets you know that apart from solid matter there is the concept of non-material thought, a sluggish process with a faint trace of awareness. Its function appears to be the appreciation of all this solid matter. Now you have two separate concepts, the material world and the awareness of it. Thought itself has to be created from nothingness as do all other concepts. Nothingness has to be the origin of all creation. The reason why people can get no further than this point is their inability to conceive an alternative to the concept of time.

Time is part and parcel of matter, space, motion and thought. When did time begin? What was there before that? What is beyond the point where space ends? All you can possibly know through the senses is what you can see, hear and touch. Beyond that you only know what you are told without actually knowing if it is true or not. (*See* Time, Space and Motion)

The seekers of origins are tied to the belief that that they can rely on the physical senses and thought's interpretation of those senses. To find the elusive answers to important questions it is necessary to transcend the senses and thought itself. Existence is completely unified consciousness. Can you visualise total nothingness? Try. This apparent nothingness is true existence or real reality. Picture some kind of gateway through which non-existence is created. There is a point of consciousness expanding in all directions. It forms a sphere of free will permeated by the essence of the original nothingness.

The creation gives rise to movement which in turn gives rise to space and the time taken to traverse it. The conscious will has equal access to existence and non-existence and has the freedom to pursue either. All creation is a blank sheet on which the free will has the ability to create its own reality. The pull of nothingness is felt throughout creation. The contradiction of non-existence manifests as a world of opposites, an is –is not scenario. The free will creates illusions. This local illusion is a world of three dimensions consisting of opposites such as positive-negative, male-female, top-bottom, front-back, right-left, hot-cold and light-darkness. Colours cancel out to return to white light.

There are also opposing concepts such as truth-deception, possession-loss, pleasure-pain and kindness-cruelty. The combined concepts shunned by those in denial add up to truth. The combined concepts embraced by them add up to the denial of truth. All possibilities manifest within the fermenting mulch. The acknowledgement of the original pull and the denial of it are the two prime aspects of the duality. The part in denial creates the concept of satan and embraces only one side of the duality such as pleasure, possession, deception and cruelty. It creates for itself a reversal of reality. They shun pain, loss, truth and kindness. The embracing of only one side of the two-sided coin keeps the two opposites apart. Only true sacred impulses do not have another half as they are a complete oneness in themselves. If you turn from pleasure and embrace suffering you reunite the two halves and find the nothingness where they cancel each other out.

You would like to know the reason why it all began but if the question is wrong the answer won't be right. There was no beginning as such, as in reality, time does not exist. Eternity does not mean a time which stretches on forever. The concept of time is a personal psychological condition which lasts only as long as your present dream. Eternity is not any kind of time, either momentary or everlasting. It is a timeless state of being. The concept of time is a product of thought. That is why you must go beyond thought and make the mind silent, to understand eternity. The sensitivity of the silent mind picks up on the wisdom forbidden by the thought machine. The less you think, the wiser you are. Wisdom is the appreciation of intelligence which is the silent mind without an agenda.

Look at the mess around you and at the ones who create and maintain it. All this, all the corruption and the pain it causes others appears to exist but does not. There is great beauty in creation, created by those who acknowledge the pull of truth. There are many diminished awareness's looking at it through the distorted psychology of the psyche, which taints it with the ugliness created by those in denial.

The great majority of individuals are inclined towards truth but there is an ever-increasing number of those in denial who are in positions of influence. Pity such individuals as they will never know the beauty which awaits you and all those who strive for truth. As you finally abandon all thought and enter the gateway of limbo you become one with the origin of all creation. The spark of awareness which seeks truth swims against the flow of the outward thrust back to the origin of pure consciousness. It is the return from the asymmetry of all possibilities to the perfect symmetry of the original sphere of conscious creation and back to the infinite stillness at the centre. The majority go with the flow according to the dictates of the psyche. The spark in denial swims with the flow into the evermore fragmented complexities of chaos. Only nothingness can be indestructible. It is beyond everything, even logic. Logic is just a signpost on the rocks of deception and self-deception, pointing the way, a beacon of light.

D

Death

You have been fed the concept of death as the absolute endgame on the chessboard of life. This could not be further from the truth. There is no such thing as death, just change within creation. You go from one condition to another till you find the truth and end all conditions. Just as you wake from a dream you wake from this present dream of a waking life. Some ask why there is no contact as proof from those who have died. This can be answered by another question. When you wake, do you go back into your dreams? Under certain conditions some do make contact with this life again, as on rare occasions you manage to slip back into one of your dreams.

You never die. You just go on till you wake to find eternity. There is no religion in eternity. There is no freedom in religion, only nonsense, fragmentation and pain. Eternity is the ultimate freedom from not only your personal creations but from all creations. Non-existence does not know or suspect what infinitely indescribable beauty existence holds.

Demons and Human Suffering

Life on the planet earth is in turmoil, as it is temporarily in the grip of opposing mental forces. These forces are not good versus evil, as many would have you believe. The so-called struggle between good and evil is a myth, a false concept. There cannot be such a concept. The concept of good represents truth. The concept of evil represents denial of that truth. Truth is not in conflict with anything. Truth just is! The denial of that truth creates all conflict within itself. In other words, the only conflict is evil versus evil, or, in mental terms, confusion versus confusion.

The astral or mental realm governs the physical realm. All movement in the physical is preceded by movement in the astral or thought realm. There are other influences from beyond the astral realm, but they are listed under another subject. (*See* Reawakening to Consciousness.)

This chapter is only concerned with the plight of the human psyche and the causes of conflict. The astral realm has all possibilities. No matter how far you stretch your imagination, your constructed dream is already there, --all the fun of the fair! The denizens or thought-forms of the astral are of all natures and tendencies. Similar forms group together in this constantly fermenting mulch. There are endless concepts. Two of these are good and evil. Those thought-forms, or psyches which are inclined to seek the truth of it all, come into the category of good. (*See* Humanity.)

Those most in denial of truth come into the category of supreme confusion, or evil. Then there are the innumerable shades of grey between the extremes, which form their own groups, with 'loose cannons' on their peripheries. The local environs of the overall mulch are vulnerable to predatory psyches, or demons. Demonic predators wallow in every perversion and wickedness imaginable, and many more unimaginable. They will prey on any vulnerable psyche. Humanity is just what the doctor ordered. (*See* Psyches.) Disembodied demons have a huge intellectual ability, but not a trace of intelligence. (*See* Intellect and Intelligence.)

The legends of mythical creatures are the result of interdimensional activity by alien entities of a satanic nature. The perceived shapes are an accurate portrayal of the satanic auras as they penetrate the sacred vibrations of this physical realm. The perceived images perfectly reflect the particular psychic vibrations of that satanic entity.

Although there are many emotive words in languages, there are also many thought-forms devoid of any linguistic connection. There are pure thought-forms which exude varying degrees of vibrations, or bursts of energy, literally thought as food. The most powerful of these bursts of energy are the involuntary ones. They create turmoil in the psyche, which loses control and gives out every last vestige of its essence of being. Nothing furnishes this supply more efficiently than physical and mental torture. Demons have brought this to a fine art. To put it bluntly, your suffering is their ecstasy! Their earthly minions tell you your particular god never gives you more suffering than you can endure. (How very kind). The opposite is true. The whole point of creating the kind of suffering on which demons feed is that it must be unbearable. Demons are not interested in stubbed toes or paper-cuts. They demand extreme torture which goes way, way beyond endurance before the victim is finally dispatched. They crave every last vestige of essence from each victim. If the population of earth were to be made aware of the lengths demons and their underlings go in their quest for ever more sophisticated forms of torture, there would be such an outraged response that the planet would literally shudder and a mass radical action would follow. (*See* Chapter 5.)

Apart from ghastly experiments in underground torture-laboratories, where tens of thousands of missing individuals end up, there are the ones so obviously in your face, you cannot see the woods for the trees. Your psyche is being tortured twenty four hours a day, seven days a week, without even suspecting it! It is misery, the most subtle of tortures, the constant stultifying and battering of your own sensitivities. This is the very essence of morbidity, a condition in which you are totally unaware of your present predicament, or your real potential.

You have been born into a planet where all events are ultimately orchestrated by stealth, according to the whims of a cluster of thought-entities. Normality is all but forgotten. It has been stolen and replaced by an obscene social structure, where intelligence is regarded as a defect and all manner of lunacy is openly tolerated. Humanity has been inveigled and coerced by stealth of cunning into accepting the unacceptable. You are a slave to the obscenities which surround you, and you are unaware of your birth-right, which is to be totally free to be an individual, savouring the fruits of a perfect utopia, --to consciously know heaven on earth. The word travesty does not even begin to describe this pain-filled cess-pit they have created. (*See* War).

Refuse to heed this warning and your children will inherit all this pain and more. You are constantly emitting a type of food that strengthens demons. Every negative thought you think is directly contributing to the immense known and hidden suffering around you and from which you so readily distance yourself. What you do not realise is that ultimately; every single individual on the planet must at some point come to know intimately the sum total of all suffering. Only such a shocking knowledge can complete your final education.

There is another type of suffering, the voluntary suffering involved in the rejection of the false identity, which is the psyche, or thought-field, in order to purify the mind. Thought-forms cannot feed on this suffering, as it is a sacred quality, the sacrifice of the false self for the sake of truth; and has gone beyond the psyche and the world of thought.

Discipline

Within the psyche the word discipline intimates the concept of authority. Inner discipline has nothing to do with any kind of authority, either that of an imagined god or the arrogant bluff of fools. Inner discipline is the freedom from all authority.

Discussion and Argument

What generally passes for discussion is an exchange of learned accepted beliefs, with each participant adhering stubbornly to their own pet theory. This is not discussion. It is argument, a waste of time and a useless noise. Real discussion is the process of communication and exchange of true feelings between any number of individuals. Each participant is prepared to sacrifice their most cherished ideal in order to clarify any question and reach a final logical conclusion for the sake of truth alone. (*See* Sincerity)

Dreams

There is the false notion put about that dreams are just a fantasy world caused by and related to events in the waking condition. Some individuals would have you believe this drivel and take money from the gullible on the basis of it. When you sleep you drift free from the daily condition you think of as waking. On waking you sometimes remember what you call dreams. The dreams you remember are just the very tip of the iceberg. There are the shallow dreams which feature trivialities from the daily routine and form a story line which ties up the mental loose ends of the recent waking condition. Apart from those there are the more serious dreams varying from the prophetic to the astonishing. These amount to a grand tour of creation and fall into the following categories.

1 - Astral projection
2 - Fantastic adventures
3 - Bizarre experiences
4 - Prophetic
5 - Lucid
6 - Recurring
7 - Morbid parallel worlds
8 - Amazing cities
9 - Lengthy dreams
10 - Meet dead people
11 - Communication with animals
12 - Worlds totally without corruption
13 - Beautiful places, situations and people
14 - Answers to perplexing questions
15 - Incredible sexual experiences
16 - Colours you never saw before
17 - Music and songs you never heard before.

When you dream you are closer to reality. There is a method for recalling them. Keep a pen and paper by your bed. Usually when you wake from a dream your focus of attention is immediately commandeered by your waking surroundings. In that moment of deflected attention your psyche loses touch with the dream you have just left and there is no overriding feeling of a need to return to that dream. There are exceptions, but they are rare.

You can train yourself to recall your dreams on waking. Immediately you wake look back at your dream and try to recall as much as possible before it fades. Ignore your waking surroundings and focus your attention on recalling the dream. Don't expect success right away. You have to be serious and work for it. Rest assured you will **succeed**. Every time you try to recall them your dreams will become more accessible. Don't worry that they will encroach on or take over your waking life. They will remain separate. Write down a few key words relevant to the dream as it will fade out before you have time for a full description. You can fill in details later. Using this method you can attain almost full recall. You only have a four second window for dream recall.

LUCID DREAMS

Tell yourself before you are ready for sleep that you will self-remember in a dream and realise you are dreaming. Whenever you think of it during the day press your fingers into some solid surface and ask yourself inwardly if you are dreaming. This is a little habit nobody will notice. Of course nothing strange will happen, but eventually you will begin doing it in your dreams. In your dream your fingers will press into the surface as though it were made of rubber or sponge and you will realise you are in a lucid dream. Don't worry about feeling silly. Remember when you enter new territory you do some things differently. When you succeed at this keep calm and try to shape the dream by doing something apparently outrageous in your surroundings. If you do not keep calm you will just wake up and waste an opportunity. In the lucid dream you can do anything you wish according to your conscience.

RECURRING DREAMS
With dream recall you will discover you have parallel lives elsewhere in creation. When such a dream begins you will have a sense of being back where you belong in a familiar setting. It is as though you carry on where you left off. These worlds are inhabited by people well known to you including your own family, not people in your waking life but in your particular dream world. In such dreams you can spend days at a time even going to bed and getting up the following morning and so on.

BIZARRE DREAMS
You can find yourself in the body of another individual and be aware of their every thought while at the same time being fully aware of your own separate identity. However, you cannot control their actions. These are usually very short episodes.

ADVENTURE DREAMS
These are extremely exciting. They include extraordinary plots and can last a day or more. They are fantastic material for a writer. One of these dreams contains enough detail for a whole novel.

ASTRAL PROJECTION (See Yoga) & MORBID WORLDS
These are nightmarish worlds populated mostly by non-humans. They are dark murky places of enforced labour.

SEXUAL DREAMS
In these worlds you meet incredibly beautiful members of the opposite sex. Their minds are just as beautiful as their bodies. You speak to and meld with these both physically and mentally.

MEETING THE DEAD
You can have meaningful conversations with well-known people who have left earth.

CITY DREAMS
You can spend many hours in a foreign city, either in this world or another. You are aware of the foreign language but are totally conversant with it. You can tour these cities and see every café, shop, cinema and note every tiniest detail. You read all the signs and smell the city. These dreams are mind-blowing and you wake up as though returning from a holiday.

CORRUPT-FREE WORLDS
These worlds are populated solely by human beings. The beauty in every aspect of these places is astounding. The peace and happiness is overwhelming. The way of living in these worlds is something to behold, simply unforgettable.

PROPHETIC DREAMS
When you wake from these dreams they stay with you with a definite sense of foreboding. They are easy to recall because of this. They are a glimpse of possible future events in the waking life. In dreams, past, present and probable future are all one and accessible. In the condition of sleep deprivation you can slip in and out of short dreams with total recall. You are aware of both dream and waking condition simultaneously. In the vast majority of cases you only have a window of three or four seconds in which to recall a dream. However, if you persist in your concentration you can extend this window, or get your foot in the door, so to speak.

Education

False education teaches the child how to be a slave. Real education does not teach the child anything. It simply shows how to be free. False education functions on belief as lies are believable, satan's bible and a guide book for the blind. Real education functions on truth. Truth is always unbelievable. Lies are for believing. Truth is for waking up to. Lies are always rushing somewhere. Truth is never in a hurry. It has nowhere to go. It has already arrived.

The Elite

There are different opinions as to who or what constitutes the elite. Many doubt that they even exist. Everybody accepts the existence of the mafia, just a local phenomenon, or local conspiracy. There are many other phenomena, corrupt politicians for example, giant corporations that gobble up smaller nests of corruption, strange, eccentric individuals and dictators. None of these are elitist, as they are all part of, or living off the corrupt proceeds of the money system, and subject to its vagaries. (*See* Money).

The real elite are faceless untouchables operating outside the money system. They have no need of money. They snap their fingers and have anything they desire. The money system is just one of the tools they employ to control humanity. They merely pretend to be part of the system, the machine. They are subhuman entities, either occupying physical bodies, or disembodied. They are totally insane, with a cunning intellect which is simply mind-boggling. Cowardice is the very core of the elite psyche. The continuing concept of cunning is the last refuge of the cornered coward. (*See* Intellect and Intelligence.)

It would be a mistake to think they are a law unto themselves, as they are outside any concept of laws. To the physical ones, earth is a playground where they amuse themselves by manipulating events. The disembodied ones want and need nothing more than a constant supply of human suffering. These are the elite. These so-called elite, as they regard themselves, are of no consequence whatsoever in greater reality. They are merely a local blip, a prisoner of their own self-importance. They are no more than a twitch in a dream, a jump in a nightmare. When it comes to the crunch, these elite would have you believe that you are their creation. Incorrect! As already stated, a human being is the eternal spirit of truth, not a DNA structure.

Today's 'elite' are the spawn of the original deniers of truth who turned their backs on the perfect symmetry of the sphere of creation. They begot their own asymmetrical world of symbols over which they reign to this day. Each of their subsequent generations have become evermore embedded in this morbid belief in symbolism. They have evolved a perverted system of numerology, the study and practice of which is no more than an introduction to black magic. They are aware of an apparent happiness which humans seem to experience and are equally aware that such an experience is beyond the reach of their understanding. Because of this, their hive mentality is bitterly envious of all humans and regards them with a searing hatred. They indulge in a constant attempt to draw the human psyche down into their spiral of self-destruction. Their thought forms hover undetected round the human aura the way the bee dances round the pollen.

The so-called elite regard the whole of humanity as their personal slaves. By stealth they have manipulated humanity into building and maintaining a fantasy world for them on this planet, which is now their comfort zone from which they manipulate the course of human affairs and feed off its many resulting aspects. The overall process amounts to factory farming.

Emotions

Emotions are the product of morbidity. They are the end result of the miseducation of the child from birth. Emotions are not to be confused with sacred impulses. Non-human controllers of humanity on earth have introduced thought into the defenceless young human mind as a noise to drown out the sensitivities which receive sacred impulses. Those true impulses are always there but are repressed because of the instilled falsehoods and attitudes fed into the psyche, giving rise to emotions. (*See* Misconceptions).

The non-human psyche does not experience emotions as the sacred impulses have been so long denied they have been forgotten. There is no conflict in such a psyche and it functions solely on automatic violent agendas and the development of cunning deception. (*See* Demons and Human Suffering).

Don't hate non-humans. Pity them in their self-created hell. The amount of harm hatred causes others is only a drop in the ocean of harm it causes you. It is a weakness and consumes your energy and true identity. Your weakness is their power. The true function of the human mind is not to function through thought but to be quiet and sensitive to sacred impulses. (*See* Impulses).

Ultimately, emotions are the result of a confused condition resulting from the conflict between true impulses and the falsehoods instilled from birth, a confused combination of the true and the false.

Establishments

The prey becomes aware of the pouncing predator when it is too late. Populations become aware of the yoke of oppression when it is too late to do anything about it. They have been warned many times but their greedy psyches mocked those who warned them and they have taken themselves and their children into an ambush. The cowardly oppressor only shows its face when it is armed to the teeth and ready to implement a programme of mass slaughter. The dream is about to become a nightmare.

The untouchables watch from the shadows. Puppet governments come and go. It makes no difference, the same establishment rules in every society. They believe themselves to be gods and have stealthily accrued power and possessions. What is important is that human beings retain their unconditional respect for each other's dignity and wellbeing.

The concept of party politics is a cunning device whereby each new government blames the one before for the never-ending injustices, thus diverting the gullible masses from the real purveyors of misery. Top politicians are well versed in the art of lying. A close study of political speeches reveals a smattering of subliminal threats. There was computer software on the market which intercepted speeches and showed this up but has now been banned by governments. The real culprits are the establishments and their bedfellows, the world monetary fund. There you have it on a plate, eat it or bin it.

Caretakers

Every establishment installs a community of caretakers till it is time for the final takeover and total enslavement of humanity. These are the so-called business communities. They are allowed free rein while enriching themselves at the expense of humanity. This situation ensures the cringing loyalty of the soulless caretakers and the control of a poverty-stricken, stress-racked and divided humanity. The caretakers are supplied with every creature comfort. They just sit back and watch an army of lackeys do their dirty work in a constant attempt to wear down and break the human spirit.

Through avid breeding their numbers have greatly increased. The resulting spawn demands an ever greater slice of the cake. The squealing piglets jostle for position as they desperately plunge their snouts ever deeper into the diminishing contents of the trough causing ever more hardship and suffering to humanity. These creatures will continue to suck the blood from the system till the whole thing collapses. By the time humanity realises what has taken place the pigs and their piglets will have quit the scene, leaving behind an empty trough.

Quangos

Unelected groups of individuals are surreptitiously assembled, whose purpose is to act as tentacles for the establishment. Any of these groups which evolve 'unsuitably' is quietly disbanded.

The Last Freedom

Humanity's only remaining 'freedom' is the concept of cash, the only and last barrier to abject slavery. A tramp, given a twenty pound note has the freedom to spend it anonymously. This last freedom will vanish as cash is done away with and replaced by a magnetic card which represents all your worldly wealth and identity in one tiny strip of code in a plastic sandwich.

Those irksome individuals who keep all the cash-paying customers waiting in the supermarket conveyer belt while they fumble with that piece of plastic, are unaware that they are leaders in the rush to destroy that last freedom, the anonymity of cash in your pocket.

Eroticism and Pornography

Eroticism is a legitimate aspect of a true society. It is totally without violence. Apart from assisting the rise of Kundalini, it soothes and fulfils sexuality. It is not salacious. It is a true art form and maintains the vitality of the sex centre. The sex centre is the super-sensitive and sacred core of a human being. Eroticism allows the full appreciation of the opposite sex, causing harm to no one. Those taking part would do so because they wished to. There would be no enticement, inveiglement or coercion involved. No need.

Pornography is the corruption of eroticism. It is produced by sub-humans motivated by greed, violence, perversion and general confusion. It is allowed to flourish by establishments in order to confuse and corrupt humanity. It has nothing to do with art and is the outright abuse of human sexuality. It does not fulfil sexuality whereas eroticism does. Any incidence of eroticism in pornography is purely accidental, as the individuals who produce it are totally unaware of the sacred nature of eroticism. Pornography degrades and brutalises the sexuality of a human being. The vast majority is produced by tasteless, talentless individuals. Their vibrations are simply not fine or sensitive enough to know any better.

The industry has been hijacked by criminals. The result is that the masses are being peddled gross, meaningless rubbish. It degrades those enticed, inveigled and coerced into taking part, thus destroying their sacred centres on the planetary level. Due to the lack of real education the majority cannot distinguish between eroticism and pornography. True eroticism would be produced by human beings who understand its true nature. It would involve a proper storyline, eventually culminating in fully explicit material. Eroticism necessitates a gradual approach to physically explicit sexual activity (the spiritual entering the physical). This instils a discipline, as in waiting for a flower to open its petals to the sunlight. In the waiting there is a gradual build-up of excitement and expectancy in the sex centre. When the final act arrives there is total fulfilment due to this discipline.

Evil Eye

The evil eye is a corruption of natural psychic ability involving the direction of negative intentions. It is influenced by demons. It operates through the emotions of one psyche to create negativity in the lives of others. However, the quality of alertness has the ability to intervene and transform a negative intention into a positive one. The developed quality of alertness has the supreme speed to step in and change a reaction into an action before the reaction can proceed automatically in accordance with the greater machine. (*See* Alertness)

Evolution

There are many types of phenomena. One does not evolve from another but remains exactly as it is within its natural margin of limited adjustment towards the origin of life. Each aspect of nature remains true to its origin if left alone. Only experimentation by external influences can cause radical change and risk diseases and deformities. Why tamper with perfection?

The concept of evolution creates the further concept of the strong taking advantage of the weak. This is not the human way of living. In a true human society the strong help the weak spiritually, mentally and physically. The non-human psyche feels the urge to dominate and control those weaker or less fortunate and labels this insidious process 'natural selection'. There is no place for the predator in reality where the lion and the lamb live in harmony.

Faith, Hope, Charity and Trust

Of the three concepts of faith, hope and charity, the first is a spiritual quality while the other two are false concepts. To have faith in someone is not the same as trusting them. Trust is the falsely created two-sided coin of trust-mistrust. With each false concept comes the possibility of its opposite, or contradiction. Faith does not create contradiction as it is a complete aspect, a sacred quality of consciousness and beyond the concept of thought itself. (*See* Creation).

So, when you trust someone, you are not paying them a compliment, but implying they may not be trustworthy, in the same way that forgiveness implies the assumption of guilt. You are telling them you are willing to take a chance on their trustworthiness. You are seeing them as a mere part of your personal world of assembled, supposedly moral values. On the other hand, when you have faith in them, there is no place for a judgemental questioning of their intentions, hence no complications, no loose ends. An act of faith makes no demands on another human being, giving them a total respect and freedom which you yourself would appreciate.

Hope is the refusal to accept the way things are. There may be hope, fear, anxiety or panic in the face of a situation but none of these automatic emotions help. Hope is an impotent condition which just eats up your energy. Things just happen the way they do, and unless you are in a position to alter the feared course of events, the results are inevitable. There is such a thing as an individual, altruistic action. This is not charity, but a simple act of kindness. (*See* Misconceptions).

Fear and Morbidity

Fear is the key emotion, the hidden emotion. The establishment of the morbid psyche heralds the dawning of fear. The morbid psyche is that which no longer suspects its own condition. Once morbidity is established the psyche becomes locked within a fixed set of accepted false beliefs. Fear is the key aspect of this seemingly helpless and hopeless condition. It takes over the life of the individual and dictates the arising of all other emotions. It becomes the datum or reference point and governs all the processes of the psyche. It is the invisible key which locks you into the virtual reality machine. It is the silent threat which holds you in obedience to the manipulators.

It takes a special courage to see through fear but like all other planted lies it dissolves when challenged. Fear functions between consideration and decision. It dictates the decision on the basis of the least painful course. It is constantly sending the message that you will be punished if you defy it. The threat falls apart if challenged but the morbid psyche cannot challenge that which it cannot define, or is unwilling to admit exists. Morbidity manifests in different ways. There is the morbidity of the religious zealot. There are the morbidities of the alcoholic, the drug addict, the serial killer, the thief, the bully, etc. etc.

Fear is the buffer which stops action and allows only reaction in accordance with a litany of planted false beliefs. All you need to do is push the cell door open and walk out but fear tells you the door is locked. Fear and morbidity are two facing mirrors which reflect and maintain each other ad infinitum. Morbidity manifests as a string of falsely created self-images which constantly change with every situation. These endless changes of management disrupt the directional flow of life, which becomes a meaningless drudge.

A message to those who think their lives are full of meaning and anything but a drudge. There are two types who think this. There are those who live according to their own conscience and refuse to go with the flow. These lives really do have meaning. Then there are those who go with the flow and try to fit in with the scheme of things. You think you are happy and content with your lot but this is only because you haven't the faintest idea of what real happiness is. What you think of as happiness is nothing more than a stultifying drudge. You stuff your faces while others starve and refuse to see the connection. You have sacrificed the treasure of all treasures for a handful of steaming crap while the unseen deceivers prepare cells for you in the torture chamber. Fear only arises in the absence of understanding. The roots of fear go deep but the shovel of truth goes infinitely deeper.

The psyche is a falsely created entity within the reality of the mind so by its very nature is an inferior entity. This entity is vaguely aware of its own inferiority and there is always a sense of something of tremendous value mysteriously missing throughout the full span of its present experience. In this condition it finds itself alone in a desert of confusion so creates for itself an oasis, a comfort zone.

It is vulnerable in the hands of the manipulators and is kept in this mental prison by a backup system of language. Apart from language the concepts of shape, colour, and the rhythm of sound and movement are used to psychologically manipulate and intimidate this already inferior entity. All this pressure creates fear through a storm of subliminal threats to the very existence of the comfort zone. The psyche will comply with any demand in order to protect and prevent the loss of this last outpost, this last semblance of comfort and peace. By its compliance the psyche effectively becomes a mere component of the thought machine.

You happily proceed with your life, always pursuing some possibility or other till suddenly everything grinds to a shuddering halt, a mental roadblock. This barrier has stopped you in your tracks, interrupted your smooth journey. Why? The concepts of possibilities and impossibilities are created and transmitted by the thought machine, the master computer. To defy an impossibility would threaten the comfort of your dream so you obey the command to stop. The concept of the impossible limits the movement of the psyche and the result is a lifetime spent in a mental tarry substance which is almost set (the condition of morbidity). In this condition constant attempts at movement eat up all your energy, leaving you worn out and broken.

What is this tarry substance? It is mechanical thought, and the only movements permitted are the ones permitted by the master computer. It's a bit like one nation being tricked into becoming a junior partner of a political bloc cleverly disguised as a trade deal. This gradual centralisation of political power into ever fewer secretive hands reduces the once free individual to the status of a slave.

You act like a robot but you are in fact a human being, a free spirit. You were never destined to lick the rear ends of non-humans, guttersnipes and perverts. There is a constant hunger for closure, an answer to that nagging sense of not really knowing the why and wherefore of your existence. The manipulators supply countless falsehoods to fill the emptiness but the falsehoods are as nothing in the vastness of the eternal void. The psyche is left with two choices. It can carry on clinging to the apron strings of some false authority or it can let go and try to come to terms with the void. Is it possible to extricate yourself from this tarry substance? For the answer read the chapter on reawakening to full consciousness.

Fictional Justice

You sit in the cinema filling your face with expensive popcorn and watch the good guys defeating the bad guys. When you leave the cocoon of the cinema you soon find out that in fact the bad guys have defeated the good guys. You have been conditioned to accept such blatant contradictions as harmless entertainment. This form of diversion is foisted on you in order to damp down, and to a degree appease your suppressed wish for real justice. You are being dosed on fictional justice with the required effect. You are paying your hard-earned money to be subliminally manipulated while unknown to you thousands of marvellous films you would appreciate far more, are being suppressed by the establishment.

Forgiveness

Someone commits a serious crime against you and you forgive them. What exactly does this mean? What would the alternative have been? Non-forgiveness? What is non-forgiveness? It must be sheer hatred, revulsion or a wish for revenge. So forgiveness must involve the suppression of this hatred. How does this affect your life? It involves drawing a curtain over a traumatic episode thus creating another shadowy department in your already departmentalised psyche. You are saddled with another loose end, another unfinished symphony.

The popular concept of forgiveness is a falsehood. It supposes itself to have an effect on the psyche of the criminal. It does not. By forgiving, you have not got rid of the hatred or urge for revenge, but have buried it where it will fester. The situation must be brought to a logical conclusion. This would involve ensuring the criminal would never again perpetrate such a crime. Face the hatred and allow it to subside in accordance with logical reasoning. Don't bury it alive. Watch it die and see it for the emotion it was. As for the criminal, see the chapters, 'guilt' and 'karma, crime and punishment.'

Faced with the crime you have two options, to forgive or not. Choosing one or the other is a form of judgement. By forgiving, are you wishing the criminal to go unpunished and continue to perpetrate crimes against others? Or is it just an attempt to suppress the revulsion within you for your own sake? Surely the criminal has to be stopped. It is not a question of punishment as such. It is a question of deterring other would-be criminals as a statement that this must stop here and now. It is a question of setting an example. This would only be an initial step to halt crime and not an attempt to use fear as an on-going deterrent. Proper education is the logical, permanent solution. To this end the criminal has to be punished, isolated and re-educated. Re-education alone can stop crime on a permanent basis.

In today's world the powers that be covertly encourage crime as a means to divide and control the populace. The establishment would lose its temporal power if it allowed proper education. The supposed act of forgiveness implies an accusation of guilt. If you do not judge you do not see guilt and there is no need to forgive a non-existent offence. Only the judgemental can forgive a perceived offence. The notion of forgiveness was invented by criminals, how convenient.

Freedom

The commonly accepted meaning attached to the word freedom is only a condition of the psyche. Real freedom has got nothing to do with the psyche. It is a state of mind. The only freedom the psyche can have is the free will to change for the better. Apart from free will there is only the continued slavery to the world of manipulated thought and manipulating thought-forms against which the psyche has no defence. The condition in which the psyche functions can scarcely be called living. If you are not totally free in every way you are not free at all. All the imagined freedoms of the psyche are transitory with a beginning and an end.

There is however a freedom that never ends and is answerable to nobody and nothing. It is the freedom from fear, authority and even death itself. It transcends the death of the physical body. It is the freedom from thought, the freedom from conditioning. It is not necessary to die to see heaven; you can have heaven on earth.

God

The human psyche has been led to believe that there is a supreme being, a god of authority in permanent residence, somewhere above the clouds and beyond the blue. You are told that this god of authority must be blindly, slavishly obeyed. If you do not blindly and unquestioningly obey, you will be sent to a terrible place after you die, be thrown into a fire where you will burn forever. However, if you blindly obey and suffer in silence, you will be sent to a paradise full of pleasures for all eternity. Well, you ask, how do we know what this god wants us to do? That's easy, we, the junior gods or priests represent god here on this planet, and it is our sacred duty to inform you of god's will. Well, you ask, how do you know what this god, who rules over the sun and all the stars, wants? You must never question what we say about the will of god. You must believe everything we say, and do everything we tell you to do. If you defy us, we will have you burned alive in a public place, as an example to others.

Well, that settled it, reward and punishment, the wages of belief! So you all lived miserably ever after. That about sums it up. Now for the truth. The only god above the clouds is a bunch of extra-terrestrials under the influence of a very foolish, demonic agenda. Authority? –the only authority is a catalogue of brutal threats and engineered atrocities, concocted in a vain attempt to enslave the human spirit. Reward? –the only rewards are petty, temporal pleasures and pastimes to keep the blind believer asleep. Punishment? The only punishment is the constant flow of human suffering on which demons feed. So much for the nonsense of this concept of a god. Then there is the sincerity and importance of real truth. You have free will. Why should you blindly believe or accept any concept when you have the ability to look at any situation for yourself? By blindly believing anything, you are effectively surrendering your freedom. There is the supreme consciousness. It is not a separate entity of authority. All authority serves one end and one end only, that of arrogance, or the attitude of the fool, one who has not the remotest interest in truth. (*See*

Authority).

The supreme consciousness includes all consciousness. It is the great collective consciousness. Every individual who ever existed or ever will has an equal share in this. At present, trapped in a condition of lowered awareness, the human mind, which has become a psyche, is unaware of its true identity as a potentially active aspect of this great consciousness. The concept of authority attempts to stifle the flow of free will. Every human being has true inner feelings and sacred impulses, as a bridge to the true identity of the collective consciousness. You have the free will to look at the possibilities, or not bother at all. There is no interference by the collective consciousness in the free will of the individual otherwise there would be no free will. The individual is a particle of consciousness, making its way back from non-existence to existence, or full consciousness. People ask: "How can an entity of pure goodness and love allow any injustice or suffering"? The answer is: "The source of all truth does not allow any injustice or suffering. Suffering does not exist! It is simply an aspect of the illusion, a journey undertaken by free will".

Humanity was coerced, inveigled into worshipping a false god. Worship is blind grovelling. How could a god of pure love and humility possibly wish to be worshipped? This would be an evil concept. They tell you that humanity was made in the image of god. Not true. The concept of a god wishing to be grovelled-to in blind worship was the devious invention of devious, non-human thought-forms. The concept of such a god was deliberately put in place to rob humanity of true freedom and dignity. Humanity is descended from the collective consciousness, which infinitely surpasses any thought-created, bullying god of myth.

Guilt

Guilt is one of the more subtle emotions, and requires a lengthy explanation. The psyche which has a very low level of awareness does not feel guilt, as it's thinking is totally automatic and knows nothing of truth. Such a psyche is not yet ready to experience guilt. The psyche which has attained a certain level of awareness may have glimpses of a greater meaning to life than hitherto known. Such a psyche knows there is a better way to live than stumbling from day to day and stopping when it is time to die. It has an inkling of something new, something worth living for, something quiet in the background, allowing the psyche to do its own thinking but subtly making its presence felt.

This psyche can choose whether to pay attention to this quietism, or ignore it. This quietism is conscience. Every moment is a choice. Once a psyche has a conscience, it is capable of feeling guilt. This is the lower end of the scale of guilt. When the psyche becomes aware of the difference between automatic reaction and conscious action, the age of the realization has dawned, and it finally knows there is a right and a wrong way to live. With responsibility comes the possibility of guilt. Once this point is reached there is no going back. When the psyche realizes it has been on the wrong road, it is aware of the choice, whether to turn round or carry on as before. When it carries on there is a twinge of conscience and guilt is born.

The feeling of guilt destroys the quality of life and eats up vital energy. With each wrongdoing the guilt builds up. It doesn't make the slightest difference what the psyche tells itself, -- deep down within its real being the guilt festers like an inescapable karma, a grim reaper at the door, waiting to collect what's left when the psyche finally succumbs to the enormous burden. (*See* **Karma**.)

Now for the important bit! You may ask if it is possible to correct this situation, or if it is possible to atone for all those wrongdoings, without having to spend thousands of years travelling through karmic life after karmic life. You will probably be surprised to hear that the answer is a resounding 'yes'. If you know you have done something wrong, meaning something detrimental to the wellbeing of others, either offhandedly or specifically for self-gratification, the spectre of guilt goes with it, whether you like it or not. If you realise this, and tell yourself that you will never do this or that again, it counts for nothing if that promise does not have a special quality. This quality is the secret for ending the nonsensical karmic reign of terror.

Have you ever made a promise to yourself or someone else that you did not keep? Think about this. If you did, there was a special ingredient missing from the promise. That ingredient is sincerity. Without this ingredient your life is a wasteland. When you make a sincere promise, you will know the difference. An empty promise is worthless, but a sincere promise ceases to be a promise and becomes a decision. When you make a real decision, nothing will make you go back on your word. When you make a decision, you have separated yourself from the past, and guilt lives in the past. In that moment guilt will be dissolved. Such a decision is a fully conscious action, where the past ceases to cast a shadow over the present.

It is a new beginning and you are a new individual, free of the hanging sword of karma. The absence of guilt will cause a huge increase in vital energy. A decision is much more than a promise; it is a cast-iron state of consciousness, knowing fully why that decision was taken, and knowing that it will never be consciously forgotten. A decision to change ends procrastination, doubt and guilt. None of this means there is a magical escape from individual obligation to redress balance. The opposite is true. In the event of the dawning of consciousness, there is the full realization of an offence from the point of view of the victim, and the death of the self which committed the offence takes the guilt with it into oblivion, and beyond all demonic influence. All balance must be restored. When something is thrown into the air, expect it to fall down. What creates guilt is not action, but the consequences of reaction. At the higher end of the scale of guilt, there are those well acquainted with the feeling, and instead of putting things right they use guilt to justify wallowing in self-pity. They accept this guilt as part of their lives and ignore their conscience.

Healing

Individuals have been conditioned to trust their health to the tender mercies of a so-called medical profession. They do not realise how much they can control their own health. It is simply another case of pseudo-education in order to keep control over people's lives. You are inveigled into signing over your life to governmental control while the quacks in the medical profession get rich at your expense. Not all doctors are quacks, but many are no more than middlemen, peddling powders, pills and poisons for gigantic, corrupt corporations run by mass murderers and allowed to thrive by governments, worldwide.

Of course, it goes without saying that you should eat healthily and exercise within reason. You don't have to be a body-builder to be healthy. It is possible to get to know your own body through yogic practices. In the physical world, truth manifests as pure white light. Normally you cannot see it, but through visualisation you can make it real. Remember, in this creation of all possibilities whatever you imagine or visualise is already there, and by visualising it you are just double-checking. Truth bears no ill-will, it only helps and comforts those who seek it. Always be aware of your body, including the brain, the function of which is to coordinate and care for the body. Be aware also of each separate part. Mentally, feel the tingling of the life-force within you. Visualise yourself enveloped by the white light of truth.

When you suffer a minor injury, like a sprain, bruise or knock, concentrate on the pain while at the same time visualising this pain being absorbed by the rest of the body and brain. Allow the injured part to go completely limp. Mentally 'withdraw' all feeling from it as though isolating it from the rest of your body. This effectively spreads the pain throughout the whole body, brain and mind. Practise this and you will be amazed at the results. A bad sprain can be made to heal instantly, using this method. This is what happens. Under normal circumstances, as nature intended, the purpose of pain is to alert the brain through the body. The brain should immediately rush to the aid of the injured part through the process of empathy. The whole body, brain and mind share the pain of that one part. This process can be likened to weight distribution where the point of a great load is spread over a large surface area thus reducing the original weight to an absolute minimum. The healing process immediately takes over. The healing energy is abundant and super-efficient. The end result can be regarded as miraculous because spiritual forces are involved.

In this world today the vast majority of individuals are in such disharmony within themselves that this natural process is either defunct or functioning well below its true potential. When you reawaken this process through concentration of visualisation the results are alarming. When you cultivate the quality of alertness you will be prepared at all times for the eventuality of such a scenario. This same empathetic process maintains the general health and balance of mind, brain and body as one conscious unit. (*See* Visualisation.)

There are those who heal others. They are highly developed spiritually with a particular gift or insight. Putting a specific pressure on various points has a very beneficial effect in a similar way to visualisation, by drawing the attention of the whole system to the location of an ache. Pressure points also affect internal organs. These points can be anywhere on the body surface. A point anywhere on any limb can have an immediate beneficial effect on a particular internal organ. With dedicated study you can ascertain the appropriate points.

The whole physical body is interconnected via a network of nerves and energy courses coordinated by the brain. The electrical brain has the power to change the chemical structures within the body. Electrical forces can convert chemical contamination into gas which is then expelled from the system. Pressure on a point exaggerates the ache and the healing process begins. Press the point and visualise the ache spreading throughout the body. There is an immediate sensation in the brain itself. It is a sensation of a welling up of vibrations felt as a buzzing, tingling or humming. It is an extremely pleasant sensation. It is the healing power at work. Visualise the pure white light moving down through your whole body altering the chemistry and sweeping away any malfunctions.

Heaven and Hell

The popular concepts of heaven and hell vary from race to race but are basically similar. Without ever having seen heaven or hell the masses have dumbly accepted what they were told by arrogant, condescending fools in fancy dress. (*See* Religion.)

All that foolish nonsense aside, there really is a heaven. Arrogance cannot know anything about the real heaven. These preachers also tell you about hell. In fact there is no such thing as hell. It is a fabrication to scare the believers. They also tell you about purgatory. There is no purgatory either. There is just the temporary condition of limbo, the transition from illusion to reality. The whole picture consists of a temporary life within the present creation, the final state of heaven which is both the beginning and end of creation and a limbo which is the crossing from the temporal to the eternal. This limbo is not any kind of punishment. It is the final act of the free will. (*See* Reawakening to Full Consciousness.)

There is no such a state or condition as punishment. Badness does not come from goodness and vice versa. There is no badness, only goodness. Good and bad are not opposites. One exists and the other does not. (*See* Creation and Free Will.)

Think of the most beautiful scenario imaginable. Now think of the most hideous scenario imaginable. As your most beautiful scenario is above your most hideous, so is heaven above your most beautiful. Have you got the picture? Now multiply the difference by a million and a million again ad infinitum. Have you got that picture? After that you still haven't the faintest idea of what heaven is like. (*See* Truth and Permanence.)

Only the manifestation of Kundalini can allow the temporal mind or psyche to catch a glimpse of heaven. It is literally heaven on earth. (*See* Kundalini.)

The free mind can see and understand this feeling. The psyche just feels a peace it never knew before.

The higher levels of true spirituality are beyond any conceptual pyramid of authority as all concepts are illusory.

Pure consciousness holds no authority of any kind. As already stated, the total absence of power is the greatest power of all.

You will not find any white-robed elders there, nor guides, lessons or tests. All such entities belong in the astral or mental plane, which in no way resembles the total freedom of absolute consciousness.

There is no light or darkness either as they are but two more concepts.

Those who have actually seen or glimpsed the real spiritual realm will never be fooled by the fake astral 'heaven'. They know full well that there is absolutely no need to 'experience the bad' in order to 'appreciate the good'. Such a concept is simply a yarn spun by demons to trick you into thinking the astral realm is a spiritual experience. This is the ultimate 'wolf in sheep's clothing'.

There are many fake heavens. The real heaven is infinitely beyond the spiritual realm. The spiritual realm is infinitely beyond the astral plane where all the fake heavens have their apparent reality. Entering the spiritual realm is waking from the dream of the astral.

They never stop lying to you via their many networks of deception. There have been many books written about experiences beyond the death of the physical body. A very small number of these are genuinely spiritual insights. The vast majority are no more than astral experiences where the individual is trapped within the karmic game of endless suffering. These astral realms are merely recycling plants where they return you again and again to their torture chambers in the denser realms of the astral.

Those who have not yet seen or glimpsed the real spiritual realm just continue to be the willing victims of the demons of a realm that is just one of a series of regenerating stations between periods of indescribable suffering. O. K. folks, tea break is over. Back on your heads.

Humanity

There are two basic types of psyche in this apparent universe. The benevolent and the belligerent. One can always be trusted, the other can never be. Both types can occupy or control any life form, not only on earth but anywhere in the physical or astral plane. They may appear physically similar but have mentalities which are diametrically opposed. There is the false supposition that all homo-sapiens are human beings. The word humanity in this context is used to represent all well- meaning benevolent and trustworthy beings of true origin.

Misdirection and false information are of the utmost importance to the so-called forces of evil. In order to make it possible for one set of individuals to dominate another it is necessary to suppress truth. Dominant forces are programmed to deceive in every way possible. They have become adepts in the art of deception in all its guises. At present the vast majority of homo-sapiens are human beings but due to a deliberate policy of interbreeding and the introduction of belligerent seed into the midst of human societies there is now a noticeable increase in the minority of sub-human mentalities. Belligerent entities are of a predatory nature and now control a large portion of the planet. More and more strange belligerent individuals are being insidiously installed in positions of influence in everyday contact with the masses of humanity. This seed is now to be found in every walk of life from so-called political leaders to psychopathic teenagers and young children without the slightest trace of human decency. These sub-human types are indirectly encouraged and protected by their counterparts in positions of authority, an authority taken over by stealth. These positions include councils, police forces and legal systems where all the odds are being stacked against common humanity. The elite are now pushing harder for full control as they can see the mass of humanity becoming more educated as to their intent.

If you have to ask yourself if you are human or not you are definitely human, as a non-human would never ask such a question. They are too well aware of their chameleonic nature and supreme cunning.

Humility and Learning

The clear mind learns from everything. It takes from a situation those aspects relevant to internal enquiry. It then proceeds in accordance with logical reasoning. Logic is a calm collected state of being. You can only learn in humility as it is the acknowledgement of how little the mind knows to begin with. There is no loss of dignity in humility. When the psyche develops an interest in a particular subject it sends messages to the conscious mind that it is ready to learn. The conscious mind comes to its assistance by pushing answers through the gaps in the mad carousel of thoughts. The motivated psyche picks up on these and sees them as moments of inspiration.

The memory functions in a similar manner. When the psyche tries hard to recall some particular detail it can get nowhere as it is functioning alone as a cluttered psyche. It appeals to the conscious mind and at a later time the memory suddenly comes through apparently out of the blue. The answer has really come from the conscious mind. The most important questions are the ones you ask yourself.

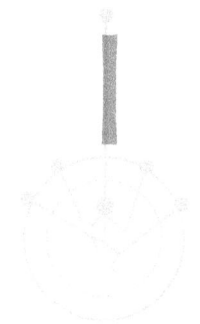

Identity

You have been miseducated and lied to from birth. Even the infant's ears absorb the bombardment by misconceptions. All the sacred knowledge which is your birthright is suppressed and withheld from the public domain. One of these truths is that the individual is not a separate brain-body entity but a spiritual being sharing all with every other being. This is the real you, a single shared identity. The controllers have instilled the idea that each individual has no responsibility for the welfare of others. They have created a dog eat dog society masquerading as civilization. This is your confused false identity. The condition of confusion consists of hundreds of separate fleeting identities in the form of emotions and learned concepts, each one vying for supremacy.

The young mind which has become a psyche functions on a stream of automatic thoughts. Every thought has a separate identity rendering the psyche truly schizophrenic. This situation ensures endless conflict within the individual. In order to reawaken to your true identity it is necessary to see the lies one at a time for what they are. Once a lie is found out it is no longer effective. You must re-educate yourself until the last lie is exposed. Then the one remaining true identity is no longer fragmented and cannot be conquered or influenced. You are no longer a slave to many tyrannies. You are truly free. (*See* Reawakening to Consciousness).

Images, Labels, Words and Subliminal Control

Almost all individuals accept labels as a legitimate part of their lives. These labels include names of people, places, objects, music and concepts. Many of them are harmless, evolved names sounding like what they represent. But some have a subliminal effect on your psyche and rule your life. The advertisement industry, which has brought psychological manipulation to a fine art use thousands of these subliminal devices. You don't have to pay attention to them. In fact, the less you are aware of them the greater the effect. They affect your thinking mechanism at a very deep level. Subliminal control is not just used in advertising but in every walk of life. It is in books, films, music, designs, speeches etc. You do not see and hear with your eyes and ears but with your psyche. Your conditioned thinking interprets incoming data according to how you were taught.

If two individuals look at the same object they see different things, each according to their personal experiences. They are not seeing the object. They are seeing the labels. There is an exercise which, if performed properly will show how labels affect images. This is not a parlour game. It should be taken seriously for results. All words are labels. Look at a simple object, say an empty matchbox. Sit comfortably as it may take some time. Hold it in your hand or place it in front of you. You are looking at a matchbox. The word match is used because it held matches. Remove the word. You are now looking at a cardboard box but the word cardboard only describes the substance of which it is made. Remove the word. You are now looking at a box but the word box only describes the shape. Remove the word. Now what are you looking at? You must remove each label and forget it before moving to the next. You will end up seeing an object you never saw before. Remember you are working on your psyche, not the object. It is simply what it is without labels. They are all in your psyche. The psyche's view of all life is superficial as everything is mummified by labels.

There is another exercise in the use of words. It is easy to say any word once as you normally use it automatically as part of a sentence. Pick any commonly used word. Its meaning springs automatically to your psyche. Begin to repeat it over and over. Like the other exercise this will take time and dedication. Repeat the word about once a second. Do not bother counting. Just concentrate on the word. Eventually the word will lose its meaning for you and you will find yourself repeating a meaningless sound. As hard as you try you cannot recall the meaning. It is just as though it is a new word you never heard before. If you continue, the sound will become more difficult to say and there comes a point when your efforts grind to a halt.

It is the automation which directs your life and in this exercise, that is missing, so the psyche experiences a moment of panic which is just a tiny taste of the condition of disorientation. This shows how unreliable the psyche really is. The meaning of the word will return shortly. This is what has actually taken place. Normally a word is used once in a string of other words and is totally automatic. But when spoken deliberately it is deprived of the spontaneous automatic recalling mechanism. You end up saying the word without its automatic meaning. You are just concentrating on the spoken word and not the meaning, so you lose touch with it. This is a yogic discipline.

A series of words or digits is repeated every day for seven days over the radio. It is broadcast again on the eighth day minus one in the series. To any psyche which listened to or overheard the broadcast, the missing word or digit will register at a deep level due to the subliminal conspicuousness of its absence. This missing word or digit is on the automatic recall system and goes to work on a deep level while the rest of the psyche is kept preoccupied and is too busy to notice. It sends a silent command to the reactionary mechanism. The psyche, being departmentalised, has one department working against another without any general awareness. This is precisely how your psyche is being spoon-fed every day and night of your life. Any message or command can be sent in this fashion. There are many more methods used to control you.

Imperceptibility

To begin with, the conscious mind functions on spontaneous and sacred impulses which have nothing to do with thought. When the mind chooses to entertain the concept of thought it becomes automatically subject to its vagaries. Every thought is but a component of the great thought machine, a virtual reality world which induces morbidity by stealth. Once caught up in the process, the lowered awareness of the psyche is easily led from the 'straight and narrow', the discipline of real being. This original discipline, the magic of consciousness, is soon forgotten.

As the awareness decreases it is drawn down into a spiral. The further you descend into the spiral the more difficult it becomes to retrace your steps. Each worsening condition wipes out the memory of previous ones. Constant changes occur, the accumulation of which eventually bring about a new condition, leaving no connection to previous ones. On a winding country road you can only see the section between the bends. The scene changes imperceptibly.

Impulses, Urges and Music

The clear mind functions according to sacred impulses from the source of creation. The psyche functions on automatic urges due to the confusion of a greatly lowered level of awareness and the encroachment of the thought process into this weakened condition. Both mind and psyche receive sacred impulses. While a clear sensitive mind directly receives them, the psyche is blinded by the inner conflict of thought which drowns out the sensitivities.

The psyche is receiving messages twenty four hours a day. It is flooded with false concepts which give rise to urges. Thought converts them into words and reactions. Sacred impulses are occasionally sensed if there is a gap in the stream of associated thoughts. It's a bit like a pedestrian trying to cross a busy road. If the traffic is heavy the chances of getting through are almost nil.

The controllers use the media to ensure the psyche is overloaded with thoughts in the form of so-called expert's reports, meaningless surveys, needless advice, tenth-rate entertainment, meaningless gossip, concocted controversies and so on. The concept of a nanny state is circulated in order to divert the attention of the masses from the fact that it is a police state. All this nonsense keeps the psyche chock-a-block with false talking points which stifle any real meaningful conversation or discussion.

Music has been hijacked and turned into a weapon. Perverted music is used to promote violent cultures among the vulnerable young. This drivel becomes the secret subliminal education of children. Peer pressure and bullying are allowed to thrive in order to cement the effect. Music can be made to recall any emotion or memory. Real music was composed in such a way as to promote positive living.

There is an experiment which proves beyond any shadow of a doubt how speech can be and is fed into musical sounds. Every single sound is a musical note. It is commonly believed that a popular song consists of just two aspects, the words and the instrumental accompaniment. This is not true. There are three aspects, two overt and one covert. The two overt aspects are the words and instrumental accompaniment. The covert aspect is the second set of words hidden in the accompaniment. Whether intentionally or not, there are always words hidden in music. If unintentional, the words are totally random. If intentional, they can be arranged to make statements, suggest ideas or trigger memories or reactionary urges. The young psyche is susceptible to the maximum influence of such subliminal aspects.

If you take any piece of recorded music and play a half-second section repeatedly, you will hear an actual word. Normally in the general flow of the music the end of one word blends in with the beginning of another and fly past so quickly they are not detectable except in the deeper levels of the departmentalised psyche. When tiny sections are isolated and repeated, the words are clearly heard. This does not just apply to music but any repeated sounds, as all sound is music. If you saw through a piece of wood you become aware of the words in the sounds made by the forward and backward strokes of the saw. Your awareness of the words is due solely to the repetitive nature of the sounds. Unknown to the population at large this technology is being used in every walk of life. With the aid of computers it is extremely efficient and effective. Secrecy and denial is necessary as this method of control can only function covertly.

The deeper levels of your psyche are always open to subliminal suggestion. If you wish to counteract such hidden activity within the psyche you can send in your own protective suggestions. This is how self-hypnosis operates. Such protection can take the form of an appropriate mantra. The mantra can consist of any number of words. Carefully construct your mantra then simplify it. Construct a short coded version of the original. Take the first letter of each word and make one word from these in any order. This new word, (it may be an invented word) will still have the full effect of the original as you alone know the true meaning. The overall intention will establish protection. Just repeat the word in your mind while visualizing yourself encased in healing protecting white light. (*See* Yoga, Visualization.)

The final mantra can consist of just one short sound. It still retains its full meaning and effect.

Innocence

Innocence is the sacred state of mind without guilt. The morbid psyche does not understand anything outside of its own gridlocked mentality so regards such a mind as easy prey. Innocence is not a lack of any kind of education or experience. It knows all it needs to know and will not allow false values to be foisted upon it. It knows it is not responsible for the mistakes of others and it knows they don't know any better. If vulnerability is the price to pay, so be it. The morbid psyche, being trapped in a violent world of reverse education regards the innocent mind as weak. The opposite is true. There is no place for cunning in the innocent mind.

Intellect and Intelligence

Intellect and intelligence are two totally separate concepts with nothing in common. Intellect is a well-oiled function within the field of thought. It is a mechanical process which can tackle mathematics, language or problem solving but cannot approach important moral issues. An intellectual individual may or may not be intelligent. There are many intellectuals who do not know right from wrong.

Intelligence does not fit into any scheme of things. It is a totally free spiritual insight. It is not tied to any race, society or cult. It is the action of a totally free mind. It is seeing life as it really is and its only concern is for the well-being of every individual on earth. Intelligence has no agenda. It is not a function of thought. It is a pure state of knowing right from wrong, a truly sacred state. An intelligent individual may or may not have high intellectual development. This is irrelevant as it does not require a high intellect to know the basics of a right and a wrong way to live.

Those who champion the concept of artificial intelligence are either knowingly or unwittingly part of an agenda to dismiss from the everyday intellect the unacceptable fact that there exists something infinitely greater than itself. There is only one intelligence, real intelligence.

Those who drone on about the possibility of creating artificial intelligence do not realise it has already been invented eons ago. What started out as artificial has become accepted as real and is known today as intellect. The phenomenon of intellect could never be remotely compared with real intelligence. Intellect is simply a mechanical reaction to the surrounding automation within the thought machine. The morbid psyche is restricted to the limitations of the mechanical intellect. Real intelligence does not 'evolve'. It is, was and always will be totally complete and at one with absolute truth.

Those who speak of (IQ) intelligence quotient are really referring to an intellectual quotient. There are many degrees of intellect but only one intelligence, which is immeasurable.

Interpretation, Humour and Laughter

Your whole life is based on interpretation. Misinterpretation is the result of miseducation. The same data is there for everyone but each one has a different interpretation based on the individually imagined reality due to the acceptance of the thought process. Is it logical that two look at the same thing and see different things? The wrongly educated psyche jumps to conclusions. It is not a question of finding the right conclusion. All conclusions are wrong, period. Thought is a very slow process and trips over itself in its haste to find a conclusion. It grabs at the most convenient one to hand. There is the individual inner interpretation and the misinterpretation in communication. The inner interpretation causes chattering in the psyche which drowns out the silent inner sensitivities. The misinterpretations in communication cause what you call misunderstandings. These render defunct any attempt at real communication.

Humour is the absence of attitude and is the awareness of misinterpretations. This awareness is usually suppressed and hidden away in the departmentalised psyche. Much comedy is based on misunderstandings and gives rise to the phenomenon of laughter. Comedy is based on the element of surprise. It highlights aspects of concepts hidden in the psyche. The sudden realization of the awareness level gives rise to laughter which is the release of pent-up stresses. Laughter really is a very good medicine.

Non-human individuals have no sense of humour and can only take pleasure from the misfortunes and suffering of others. They sneer rather than laugh. They refuse to acknowledge the existence of psychic misinterpretation. They instinctively avoid laughter for fear of vulnerability. There is the striving to dominate others and deny their own misinterpretation of life. This psyche is resentful if it is made to laugh as it thinks of everything in terms of dominating or being dominated. An attempt to make it laugh is interpreted by such a psyche as a subtle form of domination because humour highlights the weaknesses of the psyche and brings it face to face with its own ineptitude. The human psyche is willing to accept a level of humility which the non-human refuses to acknowledge.

Introspection

Introspection is a critical journey through the jungle of the psyche, an impartial study of the thought process. Its purpose is to establish a sane logical point from which to begin an enquiry into the why and wherefore of existence. In order to see clearly it is necessary for the last shred of thought to be put to rest. The psyche is a minefield of conflict and self-deception so a state of alertness must be established. This alert state is the overseer or guardian of the mind which strives to keep thought at bay. A point is reached where the last shred of thought including the false sense of ego is abandoned to leave the mind empty and silent. The mind has shed all the conflicting identities of the conditioned psyche leaving one real identity. From the silence of this one indestructible identity a meaningful enquiry can begin. True introspection is never in any way an 'ego-trip' as it must be utterly selfless.

J

Judgement

By standing on a pedestal and judging others you bring that judgement back on yourself. You will not be judged by any god or other entity but by yourself at some point on your journey of self- perfecting. Judgement is a false concept. It is born of an arrogant attitude which refuses to accept others as equals. It may be argued that devious individuals can and should be judged by decent human beings. In a normal society such individuals would be dealt with in an appropriate manner which would have nothing whatever to do with the concept of judgement. Every aspect of life is totally unique. Instead of judging, cherish that difference. In the face of negativity try to understand and introduce a positive aspect into the situation.

Karma - Crime and Punishment

The mind which allows itself to be led by others is led to believe it has no choice but to go through a process they call karma. It is told the reason for this is to have different experiences with the end-game being self-perfection. Over thousands of years under the karma system crime and atrocities have increased greatly and human suffering has increased proportionally. So what has been achieved? Who has been perfected? The concept of karma has to be examined in detail under the microscope of logical reasoning in order to establish its true nature and purpose.

A mind which thinks for itself and functions through logical reasoning can see right through all the deceptions within the karmic set-up. If a mind seeks truth for truth's sake it has no need of this nonsense. It knows it can perfect itself here and now without the need of a promise of a tomorrow which never comes and never will. Nothing happened yesterday, it happened now. Tomorrow does not exist. Everything happens here and now. The mind is born into this aspect of creation free of all concepts including the concept of karma. It is tricked into a belief system where confused emotions take the place of logical reasoning and is caught up in a web of lies. If a mind has been the victim of these lies for many years it must unlearn them by seeing them for what they are if it is to cleanse itself of the nonsense and return to the point of sane balance in which perception is crystal clear. Only then can the mind be free of the false sense of guilt which goes hand in hand with the idea of karma.

Take a good look around you. There are monuments everywhere erected to mass-murderers and perverts hailed as heroes. Governmental cover-ups which are evermore defiantly blatant. Morbid architecture of supposedly religious buildings covered in stone carvings of the ugliest monsters imaginable. Coats of arms and family crests hinting at a mixture of human and animal genes. The overpowering obsession with images of inter-bred animals, symbols and morbid rituals, secret societies and cults. All this morbid ugliness watches over the landscapes of the whole planet, yet nobody ever questions it. The collective effect of all this on the human psyche is enormous. It is the most powerful form of domination, subliminal domination. When there are aspects of life unknown and unquestioned they create a dark area in the psyche.

To the psyche, the unknown is always sensed as a hidden danger or threat. It is automatically accepted as somehow greater than the psyche as it represents that which the psyche does not understand and is subliminally accepted as superior. The unknown casts a permanent shadow over the life of the psyche. This shadow is kept in place by the maintenance of secrecy, thus creating the condition of morbidity in the human psyche and a fear of questioning anything.

The earth has been managed in such a way as to demonstrate several facts clearly. There has been and still is the deliberate orchestration of prolonging human suffering. Why should the population of any planet punish itself so terribly? Why all the savagery? In fact, why should they punish themselves at all? All this suffering cannot be the way to live. So what went wrong? Could it be due to some flaw in human nature? Is it greed? Is it incompetence? Is it corruption? Look at these questions one at a time. Start with greed. In a natural sane free-flowing human society the concept of money would not, could not even exist. (*See* Money.)

Another false concept put into circulation is that human kind is inclined towards evil. They like to call these sayings truisms, but they are anything but true. Real humanity is definitely not inclined towards evil. It is the predatory psyche which is not just inclined towards evil but is the very essence of evil insofar as evil can exist within the illusion of creation. In a natural society there would be no authority of any kind, no rules or regulations, no thin end of a wedge which could be open to abuse by any individual. Life would proceed, not according to the will of the few, but the will of everybody all the time. All viewpoints would be heard and listened to. No one would be ignored. A real sane society would function on a humanitarian basis, not a non-humanitarian, alien monetary system as at present. In the isolated event of a 'crime' there would follow natural free-flowing priorities. The victim or victims would be helped, the wrongdoer apprehended, isolated from daily life, assessed, re-educated and reassessed. Every case would be dealt with on merit as an isolated incident.

Now a message to those who would say such a society would be boring, mechanical, stultifying and unworkable. On the contrary, it would be the exact opposite. The amazing talent and skills of humanity would be fully appreciated and shared by all. The true diversity of planetary life would blossom and flourish. No place for predators. It is the present condition of so-called living which is boring, mechanical, stultifying and unworkable. What could be more stultifying than starving to death, being tortured, smashing your head against a wall in one of their asylums or committing suicide because of abuse, drugs or traumatic disillusionment. Do you really prefer this to a truly free life? If so, is it because you don't really give a damn about the suffering of others as long as you can grovel for the crumbs that fall from the tables at the banquets of the elite who police the asylum? Or are you just confused by their lies? It is time to wake up and look at yourself. End of message.

Could the cause of today's chaos be incompetence? Again, an incompetent individual would be so vastly outnumbered by competent ones that sanity would always prevail. If the majority of humanity was incompetent it would be extinct long ago, having tilted the delicate balance of nature (*See* Humanity). In human nature, as in all other nature, there are inbuilt checks and balances. These balances are more than capable of countering the effects of any imbalance within the tiny margin of adjustment. It would appear on the face of it that these balances have somehow failed to fulfil their function. This is not true. All the checks and balances are and always were in perfect working order. So who or what is responsible for the present human condition? Certainly not humanity. It is a fact that left to its own devices; humanity would have created a 'heaven on earth' where the concept of crime would never be tolerated.

There have been many perfect societies on earth which have been invaded by external disruptive influences and whole peoples exterminated. Others have been infiltrated and destroyed from the inside by covert activity, the introduction of diseases, etc. All perfect societies are a threat to the agenda of the predator. All the chaos and corruption has been introduced through stealth by disruptive predatory elements from another astral or mental realm. The unwitting agents of the elite tell you about this great game of karma. It goes as follows; You are having a hard time of it in this life so they say you must have been a right bastard in some previous life. Now you not only have the suffering to contend with, they have saddled you with a false sense of guilt as well. So far so good. The plot thickens. Now you must suffer on in order to burn off all this nasty imagined guilt. These freaks have actually got you paying for crimes you never committed.

Of course the real guilt lies with those warped morbid mind-sets which spread the lies down through all societies from the top where they orchestrate all the crime while you do all the suffering. Beautiful isn't it? You are led to believe that all these billions of individuals are suffering in silence without batting an eye. Not true. A great many do have the courage to speak out for the sake of what they know to be sane and just. These are systematically and efficiently exterminated like ants on a kitchen floor. These atrocities are carried out with all the finesse of a cold-blooded reptilian viciousness. So who is benefitting? Not humanity. But how did so many allow such a scenario to develop? The answer is simple. The manipulation of humanity has been accomplished by beings of a very different nature to humans and with a very different agenda. They have developed a rabid mechanical cunning. Within the nature of true human society there is no need for the concept of cunning as this only functions as part of the deceptive predatory psyche.

The predatory psyche, with all its highly developed cunning, preys on the innocence of human children. The predator is also a coward as it will in every case back away from a confrontation with a clear adult human mind. This is why the child's mind has to be tricked into the mechanical thought-field where it becomes a psyche, and no match for the cunning predator. The predator does not have finer human feelings and will go to any lengths without exception to accomplish any particular agenda as part of a greater agenda. Humans have been controlled by self-perpetuating lies to such a degree they unwittingly and slavishly police themselves and each other, primed and ready to betray or even kill each other at a given signal, subliminal or otherwise.

In order to scrutinise any concept it is necessary to expose one lie at a time till nothing remains but the bare bones of the situation as it really is. It is only important what you think yourself and not what some smart alec tells you. It is not a question of whether karma actually functions within the illusory process. It is a question of what it really is and why it is there. Crime is a trick. Karma is a trick. Make no mistake, the idea of karma is very cunning and appears very plausible and is all too real for those unfortunate enough to be sucked into the web of lies. What matters here and what this is all about is the real reality beyond the illusion. All these minor aspects of creation must be looked at in order to tie up the loose ends, clear out the grey areas of the mind and proceed with the real business of allowing the mind to discover its true identity and see beyond the illusion. The good news is that you can perfect yourself here and now without having to go through their falsely-created torture chamber, their karma game.

You can experience real freedom for the first time in your life and see for yourself the amazing beauty of the reality they have kept you from seeing. The predators themselves are totally unaware of real reality. If they had the faintest glimpse of reality they would instantly abandon their pathetic ravings. But alas they are buried under a mountain of lies and denials and are blind to all else. They can only function within that self-created limbo of morbidity and are controlled by their predatory nature in a never-ending search for a comfortable place in hell. Suppose you committed a crime in one life and went to another to pay for it. What would you have learned from this scenario? The reality is this. You would be paying for some crime or crimes you cannot even remember. Would it have stopped the crime? No. What has been accomplished? Nothing. All suffering is a direct result of crime, not crime in some other life but crime in the same life. Crime and suffering are tied together, one and the same process. One individual commits the crime and one or more individuals suffer as a result. And it all happens in the same life. Stop the crime and you stop the suffering. There is no need for the fairy tale about events in one life supposedly affecting another life. The simple truth is that only this life affects this life. What type of a psyche would raise objections to a utopian society? Two types would.

1—The confused psyche would object, giving all sorts of imagined reasons why it would not
work.
2—the demonic or predatory psyche would object as it is diametrically opposed to any form of peace or freedom, or the concept of a free human society living in serene happiness on a beautiful trouble-free planet.

They say you must go from life to life as part of an on-going process. They are attempting to reduce the glory of love and life to a game of snakes and ladders. This is a ploy to keep you in darkness and despair. In fact life is a completely new beginning and every moment in life is a new beginning. There is a saying; 'each moment is the beginning of the rest of your life' this is not quite accurate and should be rephrased; 'each moment is the beginning of your whole life' if there is to be radical change, your new life no longer relates to your past. Everything begins here and now. If not, you are dragging your past with you like a weight around your neck, and your every move is based on conditioned memories and associations. If you are not in control of your own mind you cannot make that new start.

Take a look at their prison systems here. Crime and criminals are big business. There is a far more sinister reason which will be mentioned later. As you may have noticed, there is no real true attempt to stop crime. All you see around you is crime and punishment ad infinitum. This propped-up status quo creates the perfect excuse for the maintenance of a massive heavy-handed police force. The human psyche functions in the astral or mental plane where anything and everything is possible. On the death of the body the psyche does not go anywhere. It simply remains in the astral where it was all along. But it is still trapped in the web of lies it believed in the 'life' just ended. The accumulation of these accepted beliefs determines any further phenomena experienced by that psyche.

On the one hand there are all these billions of crimes and on the other hand there are billions suffering in slavery. The vast majority are not even aware they have been enslaved. A bit of a merry-go-round isn't it? The situation would be laughable if it wasn't so diabolical. Like it or not, believe it or not, the truth is that earth is one huge factory-farm where the end product is human suffering. This massive suffering supplies the local astral realms with an incredibly powerful and exciting form of food, which demonic psyches gorge themselves on, their insatiable appetite demanding endless supplies, like astral junkies on a high. (*See* Demons.)

After eons of evolution, or (the automatic fermentation within the illusion) nothing in the local realms happen by accident any more. The chaos has become settled or organised into a pattern. This includes earth where the situation has assumed its present form, the organised chaos of demonology. Demons have lesser demons to do their bidding. Lesser demons have politicians to do their bidding. Where a human might take a day or a week to achieve a goal a demon can take a thousand years to achieve an agenda as they function within a different time-scale. All this doing by stealth goes completely unnoticed by humans who are manipulated with the greatest of ease. The human mind is first tricked into becoming a psyche, thus affectively causing the mind to lose sight of its true identity. Then the psyche is at the mercy of the predator. It is literally being devoured by the demonic entities. (*See* Chapter 5).

Why should you go to one life to pay for a crime in another? The time has come to stop believing in the trick of karma. Is it not logical that you should pay for a crime in the same life? Is it not logical that you would then know exactly what you were paying for? Is it not logical that you just might then have the chance to make amends to your victim and even begin perfecting yourself? Under such conditions the element of mystery would be eliminated and the scourge of morbidity non- existent. On earth, ideal conditions have been introduced and nurtured in which crime can thrive. A very tiny and selective portion of this crime is punished in order to give the impression that the powers that be are trying to combat it when in fact the very same powers are creating it. If the crime was wiped out (which would easily be achieved in a sane human society) or even significantly reduced, the heavy-handed dictatorial policing of the population would no longer be justified, the constant fear of crime and criminals by innocent victims would simply not exist, and the terrorist activity by elected so-called governments would not be justified.

Belief in the concept of karma is one of the mechanisms which ensure the continuity of crime and especially the punishment which goes with it, the mass suffering. As usual, the subliminal aspects are the most useful outcome of such a belief. The human hatred of their oppressors is to a degree damped down by the notion that they will be made to pay for their crimes against humanity in their next life by some imagined great and just god. Such a belief is no more than wishful thinking.

The same satanic psyche operates through all non-humans. It is just the masks which change, as each non-human is one of those deceptive masks and is controlled from the astral. Satanic thought- forms are not subject to reincarnation as they are tied to the astral or thought world where they work to influence the physical world.

Crime is not and never was an integral part of human nature. Within the span of an earth life you can clearly see both the crime and the suffering as one inter-connected process, but in the karmic belief system you only see the suffering, as the crime is cleverly hidden round the corner out of sight in some other imagined life. How convenient. So eliminate crime and suffering and the ideal conditions would be created in which everybody would have the opportunity to prefect themselves. Where would that leave karma? What would the demons do for food? They would be forced back into the void of nothingness which they cannot face.

They are fighting to stay in control of humanity. They are becoming desperate as they can see the truth beginning to leak out. They are determined to take over the earth before humanity learns too much. As for having different experiences, the clear silent mind can see all these different experiences and is well aware that each and every one is illusory and waiting in line like theatrical disguises for you to wear. You can go on and on trying out these disguises but none will bear the quality or dignity of the real you. All these so-called experiences are nothing more than a guided tour of the illusion and the price is your sanity and suffering. Karma is a small lie to give credence to the big lie. So much for karma. Read through this again and study the logic of it. If you are really interested, all the repetitiveness will not bother you.

Laws

Apart from the laws of nature in this local aspect of creation there are those peculiar little rules and regulations created by the few to control the many. You are a real law unto yourself but your memory of this self-sufficiency has been overridden by the clamour of foisted thought-systems. You have allowed yourself to be tricked into accepting the false laws of the few. These laws are constructed in such a way as to incorporate loopholes through which the chosen worms can wriggle. They are made complex so as to render the loopholes difficult to find except for those in the know, the bloodlines and their lackeys.

Logic

A particular concept of logic has been circulated through all societies. This image of logic suggests that logical reasoning is by its very nature a cold-blooded process devoid of human feelings. Real logical reasoning does not function through planted negative emotions or concepts, but it does function through real human feelings which are totally legitimate impulses straight from the essence of humanity, something which the manipulators have no concept of. The only cold-bloodedness is in the twisted psyches which despise all human endeavour for truth as they know it would inevitably expose them for what they are, soulless non-human entities.

Real logic is not cold-blooded in any way. It is gentle and serene. It has no need of cunning. It knows there is no cunning in the truth it seeks and finds. It is totally free of self-interest. Self-interest belongs only in the non-human psyche or the human psyche which is under the influence of the non- human psyche. Cunning is only the sophisticated practise of deception, the gateway to black magic. Logic cannot be taken in by any form of trickery. It sees a situation from every possible angle without the interference of emotions. It can see through all false concepts and lies. It's only concern is truth. Attempts have been made to confuse the issue by championing the idea of two types of logic, objective and subjective. This is complete nonsense. They claim subjective logic is a logical process in some way biased. This cannot be true as this would not be logic in any sense. There is only one logic, a clear totally sincere state of consciousness which can never be a prisoner to the thought machine with all its false concepts. It has no agenda. It is the essence of clear-sightedness. It does not rely on thesis, antithesis or synthesis as suggested by some. It proceeds on facts alone from point zero, no matter how small the beginning.

Logic travels in a circle. It begins with the question, then follows a process of elimination, double-checking each possibility against the original question. It finally returns to the point where the final answer cancels out the original question. This leaves a silent mind with no loose ends.

Love

There is the ultimate truth, that undeniable indestructability of that which is. The human concept of love is the nearest concept to describe it. All the impulses are unconditional. Truth is the collective consciousness, the total appreciation of ultimate reality. The ultimate truth has been described as pure love. In fact it is far too great to be described by any word or concept. The word love, like any other word holds a different meaning for every individual. The highest spiritual state the human mind can attain is the sacred state of pure unconditional love. This sacred impulse dissolves all sense of self-identity, even if it means death. The popular concept of love is one of total power. The popular concept of power is brutal and forceful, the only concept of power the conditioned psyche can have. The secret of the power of love is that it is none of these things. The total absence of power is the greatest power of all. The pure mind can understand unconditional love but the conditioned psyche cannot. Its humility is infinitely beyond the wildest imagination, beyond any concept of power.

Love

It is beyond time and the illusion, It is everywhere around but a conditioned psyche cannot detect it. The psyche sees what it believes to be a great variety of phenomena and concepts and denies that which it cannot see, the existence of the state of nothingness which is the closest description of ultimate truth. From the perspective of the illusion it is invisible. To find it, the psyche must sacrifice all false identity and become a pure mind again.

The secrets of eternity's design,

At last are known when opposites combine.

© 2020 (Image by Neil Hague.)

Magic

The concept of magic is not just a fantasy dreamed up as fodder for fictitious novels and films. It is a methodically thought out system whereby non-physical forces are brought to bear on physical phenomena. As the physical is already governed by the astral or thought-world it is a simple matter for those in the know to manipulate these forces. A television set or radio is a great mystery to a primitive tribe. Magic, to the uninitiated is just as great a mystery. It is just a matter of education to dispel these mysteries which have been kept hidden from the masses for so long.

The practice of magic is based on concentrated direction of willpower aided by objects or symbols or sounds. There are four types of magic, the natural magic of nature which the psyche does not notice, and three types of intentional magic.

1—The simple traditional so-called white magic which bears no ill will. It is a basic working knowledge of spells and rituals only used to help the lives of others or nature in some way.

2—Black magic is used by unscrupulous individuals for their own ends who stop at nothing to achieve their goal.

3—The real magic of consciousness. This needs no props and is in harmony with itself and the world around it. Magic actually does work.

Those who play it down most are those who use black magic. It must remain highly secret as these practices break every law both legally and morally. They have a profound effect and involve sex, murder and astral demons. Due to the immense thought-forces at work these demons or disembodied thought-forces can actually be invoked to possess a body, living or dead, or even materialise. The demon must be invited, otherwise it cannot materialise. Remember, everything is just thought, a matter of accepted belief. In this world of all possibilities black magic is a part, just one of the endless concepts of good, bad and indifferent. They all have a place in the dream.

Masculinity and Femininity

A human being does not consist of male and female aspects as some would have you believe. This false concept is encouraged in order to create confusion and further fragment the psyche. Certain aspects of masculinity and femininity are genuinely mistaken for other than what they actually are. The male does not have a female side, and vice-versa. Male and female are totally male and female respectively. Masculinity has complete respect for femininity, welcomes it with open arms into the world of the male, and vice-versa. There is complete attraction and eventual union of those equally important aspects in the full consciousness of truth. Both negative and positive give and receive each other's essence freely and unconditionally, each becoming aware of their own sexuality through the eyes of the other. Each is only concerned with the other's well-being. Like two facing mirrors, they reflect each other back and forth to infinity.

With regard to the phenomenon of homosexuality, it is a question of individual difference and not group difference as some would have you believe. Every psyche is a world in which apparent perception is no more than a projected image, leaving it in total isolation. In truth, no individual belongs to any group, or indeed any label. The gulf between a homosexual and a heterosexual is exactly the same as that between two heterosexuals or two homosexuals. Each individual should be seen as just that, simply different, without any labels whatsoever.

Groups and cults are created and maintained by those with an agenda, and not evolved by accident as is popularly believed. Each individual mind is totally unique but at one with other minds. Each psyche is also unique but isolated. A mind will never belong to any group, whereas a psyche does not belong to any group either but is tricked into the belief that it does.

Meaning

What is meaning? This transitory world is just a fleeting hypnotic dream. There is the popular concept bandied about in the world of the psyche purporting to signify some kind of meaning with which it can identify. This is not real meaning, but an attempt to fill the emptiness and sanitise the unacceptable. Real meaning is not any kind of concept or transitory condition. There can be no real meaning in such a condition, as all possibilities have a beginning and end. Real meaning never ends, as such a fate would render it meaningless and self-contradictory. If you wish to stay young you will die anyway. All acquisitions are eventually lost. You don't need to be a genius to see these simple facts.

Real meaning is based in a state of absolute permanence. It is only the illusion which is always moving, always changing. No matter what dream the individual consciousness finds itself in, this meaningful state of permanence is always accessible. It is the thread of reality running through all illusions like a string running through a necklace of beads. It is necessary to struggle free of the straightjacket of mechanical thought in order to see that meaning, but once glimpsed, it is never forgotten.

Meditation and Revelation

Depending on how seriously and deeply the psyche meditates, a point can be reached where that psyche can realise the nature of the noise or inner conflict created by its own insincerity. In such a case it can take that one extra step and silence itself. In the ensuing silence a question may be asked. The answer may come immediately or any time day or night. If the answer comes immediately well and good, so be it.

The state of silence attained by the sincere psyche is only temporary, so when it reverts back to the so-called normal condition it loses touch with that silence. It has shifted from a state back to a condition. If a particular psyche has a generally serious outlook on life it is open to messages from the silent state which it knows it once touched. In this case a pen and pad should be kept at all times in the daytime and by the bedside at night. The majority of revelations come at night when the psyche is less preoccupied and has moments of silence. You may suddenly wake up with the answer to a specific question. These flashed messages only last three or four seconds and then completely disappear without a trace. You must write as much as possible or a few key words within this limited timeframe.

The reason why it cannot be remembered is that it is received in a direct way by the conscious mind in a timeless state of silence. It cannot be captured by memory as memory is an aspect which functions only in time. No system can record that which is beyond the reach of its perceptive ability. Memory is a localised phenomenon. From the viewpoint of memory the reality from which revelation springs does not exist. It is not absolutely necessary to sit or lie down in order to meditate. Meditating is the striving of the psyche to become silent and enter a regenerative mental state. You can meditate while walking or even working. It is possible to be very active and inwardly calm or even silent at the same time.

Memory

Memory is a record of experience. It is there to consult and learn from. There are two types of memory, pure and emotive. Pure memory is an accurate record. Emotive memory is a distorted record. The clear silent mind records accurately. The psyche records inaccurately as all its incoming data is distorted by emotions, rendering it unreliable. When the psyche consults its memory record it is further distorted by more emotions, increasing the confusion. The concept of memory is complicated by the fact that it is tied to the concept of linear time. Memory does not spring from an imagined past. It builds up in the present and remains with you in the present. When an event occurs it is not left behind in some hinterland.

As soon as the psyche becomes aware of any phenomenon it is already a memory. Past and future do not exist. There is only the ever-changing now. This now contains all those things you regard as past and future aspects. Because of the mechanical nature of the world of thought all those events are fixed in a predictable dreamlike condition. The moment you wake from the dream you leave the illusion of linear time and you see all those events as they are together in that moment. When you have a premonition you are not seeing into some future world. You are catching a glimpse of a usually inaccessible part of the all-encompassing now. All the garbage shouted about an imagined future serves to stultify your enthusiasm for change for the good in the here and now. After all, lies and false promises need to be kept somewhere safe and out of reach.

Within the prison of the psyche you are at the mercy of a choiceless, purely mechanical process of encroaching memories. The psyche is being constantly invaded and harassed by these shadowy echoes of thought.

The clear mind has full control over the inflow of memories and has the ability to render each repeated experience 'ever new.' This means that the memory is never distorted by needless emotions. One of the benefits is that the same experience may be repeated any number of times and be fully appreciated each time as though for the first time. This also completely eliminates the false concept of boredom.

The free mind has the ability to temporarily blank out any section of memory, thus allowing itself to relive any experience without preconceptions. In such a case there are no negative or harmful effects as the clear mind is fully aware of every situation from every possible angle, thus never allowing any form of negativity to cloud or influence any situation.

The psyche is governed by memory.

The clear mind is served by memory.

Misconceptions

They hunted down and captured what they called wild animals, shipped them overseas and bred them in captivity. Among these noble beings were elephants who were conditioned to haul logs and perform circus tricks. After generations in captivity they gradually lost touch with the freedom of their origin. These beautiful beings were never wild, but roamed freely in their natural surrounds. The original captives have long gone, taking with them the memory of the real freedom of a life worth living. So it is with humanity. The original noble minds were trapped into becoming psyches or thought-fields where they were bred in captivity in the thought-machine. Now they number billions and have lost touch with the freedom of the mind where life was worth living.

It was necessary for their captors to create a web of lies to hide their true origin from them. Humanity may have journeyed through the stars on its way to physical captivity but its real origin is infinitely beyond the stars, beyond the physical, beyond thought itself. Once the human psyche had become established in the thought-machine it was thereafter subject to the laws of the machine. The new masters destroyed as much of the old wisdom as possible and substituted in its place a box of mental tricks, one aspect of which was the introduction of misconceptions to dazzle and confuse the psyche. All this was deemed necessary in order to minimise the possibility of any kind of serious rebellion. The rediscovery of the free mind had to be prevented at all costs.

The psyche, being no more than a computer is fully automatic and is a series of reactions to stimuli from the master-computer. Just as a virus is introduced into the computer, misconceptions are introduced into the human psyche masquerading as truisms. Here are some examples:

1—To die for a cause.
2—Humanity is descended from monkeys and fish.
3—Man is inclined towards evil.
4—Man's inhumanity to man.
5—Charity.
6—The subconscious mind.
7—Mysteries.
8—Money is the root of all evil.
9—Love is blind.
10—Making love.
11—Problems.
12—Nothing is black and white.
13—Accidents.
14—I think, therefore I am.
15—No man is an island.
16—Beauty is in the eye of the beholder.
17—Political right versus left wing.

There are a great many more but these will demonstrate their function.

TO DIE FOR A CAUSE
You can do more alive for any cause than you can dead. Billions have died in vain believing they died in a good cause. Make sure you understand the cause. Who benefits from it? There is only one possible situation where sacrificing your life can be justified. That is a situation where the only alternative is the imminent death of another life or lives. Every cause is worth living for apart from that. This particular misconception is used to justify murder and wars.

HUMANITY IS DESCENDED FROM MONKEYS AND FISH MAN IS INCLINED TOWARDS EVIL MAN'S INHUMANITY TO MAN
This twisted psychology is used to belittle the true dignity of humanity. (*See* Humanity).

CHARITY
There is such a thing as the true concept of a charitable act such as an anonymous gift or a well-meaning action totally without any expectation

of reciprocation or even thanks. That is just a basic decent human impulse. Apart from this basic decency there is something radically wrong with any society which tolerates the concept of organised charity. The very essence of organised charity is the passing round of crumbs which fall from the banqueting tables of those who have stolen the wherewithal for basic decent living from the masses. It is a slap in the face. This twisted psychology is used to give the impression of kind-heartedness while in fact is keeping down the already downtrodden. It also creates a safety valve without which the chances of rebellion would be greatly increased.

THE SUBCONSCIOUS MIND
This is a trick of upside down psychology. (*See* Psyche).

MYSTERIES
All mysteries are no more than suppressed information and miseducation to create mass ignorance and the morbid acceptance of hidden phenomena.

MONEY IS THE ROOT OF ALL EVIL
Wrong. It is not the root of all evil but just one of the tools used by the elite scum to trap humanity and control the planet. (See money).

LOVE IS BLIND
Wrong. Nothing is more clear-sighted. Everything else is blind by comparison.

MAKING LOVE
Love cannot be made. It already exists. This pathetic saying is supposed to represent the mechanical steam-engine action of a lustful male repeatedly entering a female at a rapid rate of knots. This misconception is used to degrade what is humanity's nearest concept to the ultimate truth.

PROBLEMS
There is no such thing as a problem. There is just the blind acceptance of a contradictory situation without facing it head on in a logical way. The acceptance of the unacceptable creates the concept of problems.

NOTHING IS BLACK AND WHITE
This is nothing more than a glib answer to put off further enquiry. Everything is black or white. Even the apparent shades of grey are black and white. There is a clear divide between all alternatives. Reality is simplicity itself. Everything is crystal clear. It is down to what's in the eye of the beholder.

ACCIDENTS
There is no such thing as an accident. The concept was created as a cover-up for the ineptitude of those who wish to remain untouchable. They say it could not be prevented. Yes it could, in every case.

I THINK, THEREFORE I AM
This so-called philosophy is just pure garbage, meant to be accepted by the ignorant masses as some kind of enigmatic godlike statement. All enigmatic statements are illegitimate trash meant to confuse the already puddled population. Any real information can be related in simple terms without the circus of the enigma. Truth is utterly simple. Ninety per cent of philosophers are charlatans.

NO MAN IS AN ISLAND
Wrong. Every man is an island and every woman too. The psyche, which is falsely referred to as the mind is in every case isolated, an island. This is meant to give the impression that individuals everywhere can communicate when in fact the psyche is incapable of true communication. Only a mind can communicate with another mind.

BEAUTY IS IN THE EYE OF THE BEHOLDER
Wrong. Your eye sees what it wants to see. You are surrounded by beauty which you cannot see. Only ugliness is tied to the eye of the beholder. What the eye sees is a reflection of the condition of the psyche.

RIGHT VERSUS LEFT IN POLITICS
This is another example of upside down psychology. The psyche associates right and left with right and wrong. The unscrupulous powers that be decided to class all humanitarian ideology with the label left wing to set up the wrong association in the psyche. This is a product of the non-human think-tank.

Money

The concept of money is a completely false construction. In a monetary system the most unscrupulous individuals thrive the most and use the system to take all they can for their own gratification and give nothing back to society in return. In the same system the most honest, humble and vulnerable end up as wage-slaves struggling to cope with the many institutionalised social injustices. Those at the bottom of the heap are forced to sell any valuable assets in order to buy the wherewithal to survive.

It is a conspiratorial system finely tuned to keep the vast organised work-forces struggling to keep their heads above the waves of corruption. Those who control the system surround themselves with a hierarchy of vassals including police and army chiefs. The cannon fodder which makes up these forces are the most easily led and the most susceptible to meaningless commands. The controllers are effectively selling you what they stole from your ancestors, your birthright, the beautiful planet onto which you were born with all its endless and varied supplies of food and humanity itself.

The manipulation of humanity is accomplished behind the many masks of a system of bribery. Bribery is the cement which holds the building-blocks of the money system in place. Those at the base of the controlling pyramid are held in contempt by all those above that level. They are the grossly underpaid and undervalued human workforces, having been reduced to the status of slaves and as such are never offered bribes. Bribery begins above that level. The higher in the pyramid of influence the bigger the bribes. Such bribes are disguised as expenses, bonuses, directorships, titles etc etc. Any mask will do, not to mention the bulging brown envelopes.

You do all the work. They claim ownership of all that you have produced by the sweat of your brow. You are then forced to buy back that which you have constructed, planted and reaped, processed and delivered. They contribute nothing but misery and smugly hand you pieces of coloured paper, the value of which they regulate to keep it almost worthless to you, thus maintaining the status quo. They have turned a paradise into a playground for their perverted games and have made you and your loved ones pawns in those games.

When it is required by the elite their vassals arrange a breakdown in the system in order to bring the work-forces to their knees. These breakdowns do not happen by accident. They are arranged, sometimes years in advance. There is no such thing as money. It is the biggest confidence trick in history. It is purely imaginary, a game of bluff played by the elite. The human mind which had been converted into a psyche was easily manipulated into this system. For all intents and purposes monopoly-money, while the game lasts, is just as valuable as those pieces of paper the elite print as your wages. They both have a pretended value. It is even useless as toilet-paper. The only real currency on earth at present is the currency of human vibrations, sweat, blood and suffering which are the products of the falsely created psyche which they control through the various manifestations of fear. The moment the concept of money is introduced a society is automatically doomed through nepotism.

Q. What was there before the introduction of money into human

society?
A. Everything there is now, with one exception, organised corruption.

Q. How would society have been developed without the concept of money?
A. It would have been consciously developed on a strictly humanitarian basis.

In order to further disorientate the masses they have circulated such concepts as alternative societies perceived as a threat or even a spur to war. The whole concept of communism is a trick as it's merely another form of capitalism in disguise. All money systems are exactly the same as they are all wide open to manipulation by corrupt individuals. As such they all become part of a much bigger worldwide game.

Only an alien or non-human psyche could glorify corruption or pay homage to the concept of deception. This is not, never was and never will be the way a real genuine human being would wish to live. The concept of money was created, not for the purpose of business management but solely for the purpose of taking complete control of humanity with the elite manipulators having total freedom to do exactly as they please while humanity is firmly in the grip of abject slavery. This is the ultimate agenda. For this reason and this reason alone money was created. Money systems can only function on mass poverty and slavery.

Before today's money system was fully implemented, groups were controlled through brute force and fear of punishment alone. The more hot-blooded or culturally rooted the group, the more brutal and vicious the dictatorship.

All groups were ruled by dictatorships and still are to this day. There are two types of dictatorship, the 'extreme' and the 'soft'. The difference between the two is that the 'soft' call themselves 'democracies', a system supposedly ruled by the 'majority', but is in effect ruled by a secret minority.

The extreme dictatorships still rule by brute force whereas the soft dictatorships or so-called democracies rule by the use of much cunning and psychological trickery in an attempt to reduce once peaceful, carefree and harmonious groups to 'races of idiots.'

The masses under extreme dictatorships are well aware of their enforced serfdom. These have been physically crushed.

Those under soft dictatorships have been led to believe that they are in some way free. These have been both physically and mentally crushed.

Different dictatorships are made to appear entirely separate entities, but are working in tandem through a common controller with the eventual aim or agenda of bringing them all under one worldwide dictatorship, where the full force of a long hidden technology will be released to totally subdue what's left of the human race.

In the meantime, they will use the illusion of separate states to facilitate the mass extermination of large portions of the planet's population through falsely created wars and deliberately planted infectious diseases. Those having outlived their usefulness (including the caretakers), will be thrown to the wolves. Job done.

Morbidity and the Psyche

Morbidity is the instilled fear of leaving the comfort zone. The psyche functions in a world of force-fed false concepts where it seeks solace on an island of lesser misery in an ocean of greater misery. This island is its comfort zone. It is a grey world of shadows with occasional deviations to alleviate the crushing boredom. Morbidity destroys communication as it forces each individual into a cocoon, creating isolation. The psyche numbly accepts clichéd cop-outs such as, 'well that's human nature'—'well that's the way it is' or the classic, 'it's not that simple'. These foolish clichés are the common response to an attempted conversation of major importance. In fact it is not human nature, not just the way it is, and yes, it is that simple.

You have to leave that little comfort zone to see the truth of the simplicity of reality. When children ask so-called embarrassing questions they are not themselves embarrassed by such questions as they are not yet moulded into morbid psyches fearful of these questions. The child's mind looks and questions what it sees. The adult psyche looks but is conditioned to accept the unacceptable. The child recognises the unacceptability of a situation as it is born into a world of potholes and poverty. It is puzzled by the way adults allow this strangeness to prevail. Then, hey presto, the child's mind is snatched into the trauma-factory where it is taught to be a psyche just like those big palookas.

The adult psyche has a vague memory of once being a child itself, but on it's journey through the trauma-factory has lost that vital connection with that innocent young mind. The moment the mind loses sight of that precious independent innocence it becomes a psyche. The psyche now finds itself tiptoeing through a minefield of forbidden freedoms. It is afraid to question the lies of those who hold the guns and ends up stagnating in a hopeless grey torpor where the herd mentality insists on total conformity. The world of such an individual is the condition of morbidity, a dream within a dream, a quicksand of confusion, totally unaware of true happiness or freedom. The morbid psyche functions in a world where cunning deception rules. The scum rises to the top. In a world dominated by ancient psyches far more cunning and streetwise in the ways of the dream the human psyche doesn't stand the ghost of a chance. It is under constant attack from unseen and undreamed of forces.

Everything experienced by the psyche is a trauma varying in intensity from almost imperceptible to devastating. Strong trauma produces conflict, creating no-go areas in which certain memories are hidden. Barriers are erected causing departmentalisation. This is a schizophrenic condition consisting of hundreds of identities in conflict with each other. This fragmented bundle of identities is led to believe it is a single identity. (*See* Identity).

The manipulators have kept the human psyche in awe of authority by systematically starving it of real knowledge. The psyche does not want trouble in its life so avoids upsetting what it sees as authority. Morbidity is the general feeling of vulnerability, a vague sense that something of tremendous value is missing in life. It cannot see clearly through the forest of lies it is being spoon-fed. The psyche can only function on data supplied by external influences. The clear mind creates its own data and determines its own direction in life. The psyche is totally unaware of the freedom of a clear mind. The psyche thinks and surmises. The mind knows.

Mysteries

There are no mysteries, just hidden knowledge. It is the stage magician's marvellous feat till you find out how it was done. It falls apart when it loses its mystique. The concept of mystery is in reality unacceptable but the psyche has been conditioned to accept the unacceptable and sits at the poker table playing one losing hand after another. The rulers dare not allow hidden knowledge to be divulged as this would be the beginning of the end for them. Leaks do not happen by accident. Some are false. Some truths are leaked selectively.

Don't believe for a moment that those who have carefully conspired for many centuries make mistakes. They do not. Everything is planned and timed. Any actual mistakes are of no consequence in the greater scheme of things.

Need, Wanting and Giving

The concept of need is very subtle, difficult for the psyche to grasp and requires some study. 'You only need what you have not got'. Is that a logical statement? No it is not logical. The concept of need is false. You either have or have not. The logical process is to receive what is appropriate within the natural flow of living without needing it. The concept of needing creates a negative in the psyche, a something missing. By dwelling on what it has not got it misses out on what it has. Need accomplishes nothing. It is a wish or desire for more than you have.

If you are hungry you eat without psychologically needing to or thinking you must do so. Needing to eat does not make the food any more nourishing. When you are hungry fear tells you to avoid the pangs of hunger. Don't be afraid of the pangs. Give fear the one fingered salute. You don't need or have to do anything. You simply do or you don't, thus simplifying living. The concepts of needing and wanting are the automatic reactions of the psyche in an attempt to reach out of the real now into a non-existent future. To simplify living you remain in the now with what you have. Millions are starving. They need food but what good is the needing doing them? Correct action in the now dissolves the concept of need. Subliminal advertising instils the concept of need in the psyche and keeps it locked in a condition of slavery to the distributers of crumbs. Wanting is the sacrifice of dignity, Giving dissolves the concept of taking. Why tolerate or make allowances for those who take without giving? Everyone has something to contribute to a true society and all giving is equal in truth. Don't let them sell you what is already rightfully yours.

Paedophilia

Paedophilia is an extreme morbid condition where the psyche has lost touch with any form of self-discipline. It has turned in on itself at the bottom of a spiral to oblivion. (*See* Imperceptibility).

Such individuals are either demons or have fallen completely under the control of demons. There are millions of these creatures operating in secrecy, many attaining high office among the ranks of humanity. If you have children it is wise to assume they are being watched by at least one of these predators. Be aware of the dangers and be extra cautious. Caution bears no relation to paranoia. Paranoia is a condition based on fear. Caution is plain common sense based on the plain logic of truth.

Red-eyed wolf, you've had your day,
Your time is up.
You're now the prey.
The plot's now long-awaited twist,
reveals your outline in the mist.
The sheep are coming to their senses,
Now they're tearing down the fences.
Now is yesterday's tomorrow,
No time left for you to borrow.
Too late, fool, to see the light,
Your gruesome end is now in sight.
Where you're bound you'll have no voice,
as non-existence was your choice.
Red-eyed wolf, your days are done,
You've had your time beneath the sun.
You'll leave the dream of time and space,

to disappear without a trace.
Where you're bound there's no respite,
No second chance to see the light.
In the hell that spawned your game,
your master now stokes up the flame.
You'll grovel at your master's feet,
It's now your turn to feel the heat.
It's time for you to understand,
Payback time is close at hand.
You see, it does not end in death,
There's no escape through your last breath.
After that you carry on,
Now there's a thought to dwell upon.
Not at all what you expected,
our mistakes to be corrected.
Beyond the shadow of a doubt,
You can see there's no way out.
The rights of others you have scorned,
Not as though you've not been warned.
Your light has lost its final spark,
Without a warning all goes dark.
The blackness forms an endless bowl,
A mirror of your absent soul.
The tolling of a distant bell,
An unimaginable hell.
In the ashes you'll remain,
where you'll writhe in endless pain.
The horrors pound your thoughts to dust,
You can't endure it, yet you must.
You'll glimpse your victims one by one,
where they still live beneath the sun.
A sun far brighter than before,
its brightness growing evermore.
Upon the truth you slammed the door,
so red-eyed wolf, you are no more.

Peace of Mind

What is meant by 'peace of mind'? Considering the greater portion of humanity has lost touch with its collective mind, and proceeds as a collective psyche, the term 'peace of psyche' would be more appropriate. However, it is impossible to have a peaceful psyche. Only the transformation of psyche to mind can ever bring true peace. The mind is always at peace with itself and all surrounding phenomena.

Personality and Character

Personality is the outer manifestation of the psyche. It is deceptive and prone to betray promises to itself and others. It is merely a dancing clown and totally unreliable. Character is the discipline of the real inner being and is 100% reliable.

Pleasure

Pleasure is a legitimate aspect of planetary life, the ecstasy of an eternal spiritual fulfilment, and not the constant striving for self-gratification, which is transitory and worthless.

Possession by Demons

Demonic possession is no myth, and far more common than people are led to believe. Earth is the sacred product of collective free will evolved from all possibilities. Its environs have been targeted and invaded by thought-entities in denial of truth. This invasion manifests as a thought-machine. All beings have the freedom to become involved with this machine. Involvement with this automatic process reduces the once-free being to the level of an automaton, thus inviting the attention of demons.

When a mind becomes a psyche the demon sees it as ripe for influencing. It works its cunning influence on its prey till it becomes morbid. It is then ready for invasion. A demon does not wait for a cordial invitation. Due to the total lack of real education the psyche is unaware of this danger. It is now just a vehicle driven by the demon. Not all mental problems are due to demonic influence. A psyche is always liable to go off the rails in its confused condition. There is no difference between the mentality of a morbid psyche and that of a mad dog. So beware of yourself.

Possessiveness

To possess nothing is to have everything. To share is to sow the seeds of utopia and create a paradise.

Prayer

Is the concept of prayer a legitimate function? Yes it is, but not if you are asking for trivial personal favours from a fictitious god of your imagination. The result of such begging will either be a coincidence or a placebo effect but not the real thing. (*See* God).

Why waste your time asking for favours if your god is omnipotent and already knows every thought in your mind? Instead, communicate with yourself because within you is that false god and beyond that god is the real truth, the collective consciousness. Be free of the tyranny of false gods and controllers disguised as do-gooders. Look for a truth in which there are no demands, no authority and no bowing to another's will. If you want to help or protect another visualise them surrounded by that light. Your prayer will be the intention you send with the light. (*See* Yoga –Visualisation).

Problems

There is no such thing as a problem. The popular concept of a problem is an unsatisfactory situation which creates conflicting courses of action, a question without an answer. Every question has an answer. Due to some emotional attachment or peer pressure the psyche refuses to acknowledge the logical process which gives the answer. The logical process leaves just one course of action after eliminating the alternatives.

Problems are either incidental or on-going. An incidental problem is due to some oversight. Learn from mistakes and try to be more attentive. If a problem is on-going logic asks three questions:

1 --What was the initial cause?
2 --Why was it not sorted out?
3 --How can it be sorted out now?

There is usually a corrupt motive behind an on-going problem. Organised corruption keeps the proper solution suppressed. If it really bothers you, do something about it. If it doesn't, forget it. It's as simple as that.

The Psyche and Personality

The human psyche can only function on data supplied by external influences whereas the clear mind creates its own data and determines its own direction in life. The psyche is totally unaware that there is such a thing as a clear mind. It thinks and surmises whereas the mind knows. The erratic behaviour of the human psyche is not human nature. Human nature is the proper logical functioning of the clear human mind.

When a young child is forced into a mechanical way of functioning and subjected to parental and peer pressure it loses touch with its original state of pure innocence. The controllers of society take full advantage of the child's vulnerability and ceaselessly batter its mind with falsehoods. This causes the child to eventually toe the line and in doing so the child's mind becomes a psyche cluttered with negative thoughts. It is then conditioned in preparation for manipulating as a mere puppet in the hands of extremely devious natures. When the psyche finally loses all its memories of the original innocent state it becomes morbid. It has forgotten the meaning of real freedom, and is now a prisoner of all external influences. Its life becomes filled with confusion and is overloaded by the constant bombardment of nonsense. The morbid psyche is that which has lost all touch with reality, its true individuality and identity.

Not all psyches are morbid. A psyche which listens to the sacred impulses within is not morbid and can only be controlled to a point. The morbid psyche is a confused mess which clutters your clear mind with abominable nonsense. Personality is the outward manifestation of the psyche. It is the personality which interacts between individuals. Personality does not represent the mind, just the psyche.

Psychology and Psychiatry

Problems arise due to the awareness being focused on the self. Every second you focus on the needs of others is a second less focused on yourself. Thinking of others diminishes self-concern and all that totally unnecessary worry. A great many so-called psychologists and psychiatrists profess a totally wrong view of the human condition. They have been led to believe by the teachings of the establishment that the unconscious condition of the psyche is actually a conscious state of mind. The opposite is true.

They talk about the condition of schizophrenia as though it were an illness of the conscious mind. That is impossible as the conscious mind has no illnesses whatsoever. In fact the natural condition of the psyche is one of confused departmentalisation. No doubt some of these so-called experts suspect the truth but are afraid to step out of line. They just go with the flow while raking in the money. A few are part of the cover-up. As for the rest, they are just as confused as their so-called patients.

The one and only cure for problems within the dream of the psyche is to wake up, to empty your conscious mind of all the garbage learned by the psyche through the medium of thought. You simply need to leave the machine by re-educating yourself. In the meantime try to relax as much as possible and focus on keeping calm in every situation.

R

Race

All plant, animal and human life flourishes in its own particular way. Each has its characteristics evolved from the original mulch of all possibilities. In the pine forest no two trees are alike in every detail but are closely related and function within a framework of an established agenda to retain their joint identity as a pine forest. Some plants attract each other. Some repel each other. When two adjacent plants repel each other one dominates while the other suffers or even perishes as a result.

So it is with races of people. Each race was developed originally under separate conditions. They developed particular skills springing from the essence of their collective nature. When two races are thrust together each one dominates the other in its particular field of excellence. The manipulators of planetary affairs have caused the uprooting and moving of whole populations under differing pretexts. This fact is played down by claiming all races have equal opportunities but secretly using one race to control another. Each plant or herb has its own characteristics which contribute to the overall well-being of the planet as one unit.

The knowledgeable gardener has the ability to use plants in many ways. The intelligent gardener knows the nature of plants and their potential for interaction with each other, so works in the interests of the well-being of all. The incompetent gardener may cause chaos, bringing about conditions of disease and death in the plant world. In the world of thought which has complete control of the planetary psyche, exactly the same rule applies. Differently seeded races were allowed to evolve naturally to a certain point as seeds are germinated in trays. The earth is a floating garden, with seeded life-forms seen from a distance as a covering of fermenting dust which emits powerful and exciting vibrations. The mental or astral world feeds on this. Through these emissions the full beauty and excitement of planetary living can be accessed. It is like walking through a busy hotel kitchen and savouring the smell of the many herbs and spices. Imagine this on a mental level, the thrill of the race, the many wonderful sensations, the ever-present air of expectancy and the final realisation of all the joys of living.

This combined consciousness pours forth like the intoxicating scent of a flowerbed. But it is not just the smell of natural beautiful feelings which are of interest to certain thought-forms. It is the smell of shock and extreme trauma which attracts these. Enter the dark forces, that part of all possibilities which is the dark side of the coin of light and darkness springing from the free will to explore and pursue all aims. These predatory disembodied psyches target earth with the sole purpose of converting conscious minds to psyches, thus converting serene happiness into indescribable suffering. (See *Demons and Human suffering*).

They change the scent of life into the stench of death. The incompetent gardener sets to work twisting nature into morbid shapes to produce maximum suffering for the masters to feast on. Concepts such as religion and nationality are instilled into races to divide and conquer and create the conditions for war. These concepts are self-perpetuating through fear and peer pressure. Paedophilic thought-forms are seeded and allowed to prey on children in order to destroy their natural centre of balance and produce confused and easily manipulated adult psyches. Take away religion and the race still remains. Religion is also used to rope in members of other races enabling them to point a finger and say,--'It's not a race, it's a religion'. Actually, it is a race, with a number of unwitting participants on the periphery. Just as individuals, one race is used to control another. Check it out, but whatever you do never label any one individual with the identity of one particular race. Ultimately everyone on earth is a free agent. Your greatest enemy is your own psyche. (*See* Psyche).

The sum total of all positive and negative aspects of any race is its essence. One race is used to suppress other races through its negative aspects.

Reawakening to Full Consciousness

The full consciousness of truth is simple to the point of infinite zero. The unconscious condition of the psyche becomes ever more complex as it denies the simplicity of truth. The waking process is the rejection of all the falsehoods which now fill your mind and the return to the nothingness which contains infinitely more than all the dreams which ever were or ever will be. It is simply a question of the undoing of the burden of the complexity to regain the totally restful and peaceful state of infinite simplicity. You are not here to serve an afterlife. You can have heaven right here on earth now and forever.

You see the chaos in the world. You see also that the quality of real true freedom and happiness is almost non-existent. You would like to know if there is a deeper meaning to existence than the one you are familiar with. If you are happy with your lot here and don't really feel the urge to seek the truth of it all don't waste your time with this. However, if you feel an overpowering impulse to seek the answers to many questions hitherto unanswered, and you know that this impulse comes from the still small voice deep within the very core of your being, read on.

Start from where you are. You find yourself in an astral world or a world of thought, of which this apparently solid physical universe is a part. Your original full consciousness was lulled to sleep as it gradually descended into the denser realms of the thought-world. You have become mesmerised by the physical world and have retained just enough awareness to function here. You are drifting around aimlessly on the bottom of an immense ocean of thought-stuff. Thought-sharks are swimming above you waiting to devour you. You have forgotten your origin and identity. Your awareness has stagnated and become settled in a fixed pattern of thought-processes. This is your psyche. Your psyche manifests as your personality. Your personality manifests as a fixed pattern of reactionary behaviour.

You have been reduced to a creature of habit. You are totally predictable and easy prey to any predatory thought-entities. You are being influenced and manipulated with the greatest of ease. You are trapped in this condition of enslavement. In this condition your psyche has built itself a comfort-zone to ensure a modicum of security amid a level of confusion and violence which it has come to accept as normal. You have come to cherish this comfort-zone and think of it as the real you. You are very protective of it, sometimes to the point of paranoia.

There is a system which enables you to retrace your path step by step back to full consciousness. Take a look at dreams. Your psyche functions permanently in the astral realm or the world of thought. While the physical body is functioning the psyche gives its full attention to its needs, and only daydreams at opportune moments. When the body needs rejuvenation and is at rest the psyche is free to function in many other ways in the astral. Some of these experiences are remembered as dreams. (*See* Dreams).

When the body is rested or disturbed in some way the attention of the psyche is drawn back. As you wake back to the body you are confused and cling to the dream as it represents your present reality. As the waking process takes its course you are dragged from that reality. If it is a pleasant reality you desperately cling to it. If it is unpleasant you are relieved or even overjoyed to get away from it. In both cases it was absolutely real to you while it lasted.

You are now fully awake to the physical senses again and soon forget that which you were so convinced was real and look back on it as an illusion. In fact it is every bit as real as what you call your waking state. Both are astral experiences with one vital difference. The difference is that while your psyche is totally preoccupied with the body your awareness is effectively being prevented from having visions of reality, or messages from your consciousness.

During the process of what you call sleep your awareness is free from the concepts of physical and psychological time. Often on waking to the body some of these experiences are recalled but quickly vanish, as the psyche cannot understand the real meaning of these memories. They just fade away, sometimes leaving a trace of wonder or even amazement. Then they are shut down by automatic reactionary mechanisms planted and nurtured in your psyche. You now imagine yourself to be fully awake but you are still asleep. You have simply moved from one aspect of the illusion to another and there is no alarm clock to wake you from the overall illusion. However if you sincerely seek truth there is a method for waking yourself.

This is the most important piece of information you will ever come across. Books have been destroyed and people murdered to prevent this knowledge from reaching the domain of the general population. It should be of passing interest as a read but if ever you feel the impulse, it is there to consult. As long as you genuinely seek answers and are totally sincere in your intentions this system of waking to regain control of your life can never fail. The process is far from easy but never impossible. It cannot be stressed enough the importance of total sincerity and commitment as this will be your driving force and only companion on the loneliest journey you will ever undertake. You don't have to join any club or go cap-in-hand to any authority. All the answers are there within your own consciousness. Before going into the finer details of the actual system here is a rough summary of the process.

It involves a journey into the innermost sanctum of the psyche. It begins simply and progresses by stages into the world of thought. You tread carefully in this new territory. The jungle of thought is infinitely more treacherous than any physical jungle. You will penetrate the barriers erected by the lies and misconceptions your psyche has been bombarded with from birth. Your expanding awareness will enter the no-go areas, those grey areas where the psyche, left to its own devices, could never dare venture. You will see for yourself the mechanical nature of the psyche. You will scrutinise your habits, emotions, reactions, beliefs and attitudes one at a time. As you come to realise the true nature of the thought-process you will be surprised and sometimes shocked by what you find. There will occur periods of disorientation as you begin to see your psyche in a new light. At this point you are still clinging to your false identity. (*See* Identities).

There is no rush as the process involves leaving time and entering eternity, the eternal state of now. At present, your psyche functions within an illusory frame-work where it flits back and forth between an imagined future and a dead past but never in the living present. It is necessary to eliminate the influence of a dead past and imagined future in order to see the present as it really is. You will not understand the concept of eternity till you actually see it. No harm will come to your mind or body. You will feel vulnerable and disorientated as you leave your comfort-zone, as this is the very thing you always identified with and regarded as the real you. The process requires total absence of self- interest. The only legitimate sacrifice is self-sacrifice. If you feel you are losing your mind, it is because you are, the old artificial one, the psyche, the indoctrinated thought-field.

If you become too stressed, leave the process immediately for as long as it takes to bring yourself back down to earth so to speak. Do not continue the process till you feel you are ready. Never pressure yourself. This is about ending all stress, not creating more. Your original intention to seek the truth about existence will be your constant guardian and there will be help along the way from unexpected sources. Your whole life is being watched over by the very truth you seek. It is always ready to help. The programmed nature of your psyche will fight your efforts all the way. At present, there is no resistance from the machinery of the psyche as your life is proceeding just as intended by those influences which now control you. The stronger your mind becomes the more the psyche will find or invent reasons why it is foolish to pursue anything beyond the physical.

The chattering monkeys will condemn all serious enquiry, as they are programmed to resist.

There are and always were esoteric schools for those who seek the hidden secrets of life but feel they cannot cope alone. These students of truth support each other through the unbearable condition and difficult times of disorientation. They attempt to master the mechanical nature of their psyches through self-discipline. As you progress in your studies there will be indications of your success. You will have momentary flashes of insights of different types. You can suddenly have a fleeting glimpse of the state of eternity. All your present experiences are mechanical conditions, not states. A state is the fully conscious awareness of reality. (*See* States.)

You may suddenly become telepathic. You may be overwhelmed by extreme, almost unbearable sensations of well-being or even ecstasy. You are becoming more aware of reality as you clear away all the negatives which have been misdirecting your life and eating up all your vital energy. The new insights will give you added incentive to carry on the journey of discovery. Remember, this system is not a university course. You don't have to wait for results. They are instantly apparent. You are completely in charge. You are teacher and pupil all in one. There is no authority whatsoever. (*See* Authority).

This is all about gaining absolute freedom from the clutches of the organisers of strife, chaos and pain. (See mind-control). You will penetrate the jungles of the thought-world which make the impenetrable physical jungles look like a window-box. As your conscious awareness expands you will attain new abilities and powers which you will be tempted to use for your own selfish ends. Your psyche will try to rationalise why you should use these powers. Temptation is one of the most effective weapons in the arsenal of the psyche. Remember the psyche is only the servant of its hidden masters. So be warned. On no account allow yourself to be tempted.

As you near the end of your journey you will face the greatest challenge of all, the final sacrifice of the self. You will be emptying your mind of the last shred of thought and then even the very thing which has made that decision, the self, the 'you' that you so cherished. This is the ultimate act of humility, the ultimate sacrifice, the final conclusion of the cleansing process. You have won the battle of wits with the falsely planted schizophrenic psyche. You now teeter on the edge of a void of nothingness. You no longer think. That which did the thinking is gone and you are alone in the void. But the precious knowledge which you have gained has let you know that all will be well. There is no longer a sense of self, just the void, a void so profound that even the void does not exist. The disorientation is total.

You may have read descriptions of the condition of disorientation but you will never know the full horror of it till you are there on the brink. You have just sacrificed your old identity and would give anything just to be back there in that little familiar comfort-zone with all its foolish little distractions. You are experiencing the very last condition of your life. The condition of complete disorientation. This is the last throw of the dice by the disappearing psyche. How deeply you were immersed in the illusion will determine the duration of this final condition. It is the darkness before the dawn. It may last hours, days or weeks, but the new dawn is now inevitable. As this terrifying period comes to an end the fog will lift, and when it does, a new intelligence is looking through your eyes. All of those moments of insight are now a permanent part of this new being. There is no sense of self, just a point of intelligence which is part of the all-pervading intelligence of reality. Gone is the old thought-process which functioned as a string of jumping movements in its desperate attempt to reach some convenient conclusion, consuming huge quantities of energy as it dived back and forth. Gone are all the connected associations which used to distort reality and perpetuate the morbidity of the psyche.

There is now a clear state of knowing. It brings about action through spontaneous impulses. You need nothing. You want nothing. You are everything and everyone. You see your body, your surrounds and other people. You feel the warmth of the sun, the raindrops and all the other physical aspects of earth-life, but not as the old psyche used to. It is as though you have just arrived from another place in another universe and are seeing everything for the first time. You see the falseness of the concept of time in all its physical and psychological diversity. You are aware of a silence, not a physical silence, but a mental silence. The silence is louder than the loudest noise. Where the noise used to drown out the silence, now the silence drowns out the noise.

You realise that this silence is the absence of all those chattering monkeys of thought. There is none of the inner conflict or guilt which used to keep the psyche in chains. There is a profound calmness and complete appreciation of everything. An indescribably beautiful sensation surges through your being, a sensation so utterly delicate and yet so powerful that everything else dissolves in the presence of that which cannot be destroyed, that which is. You are no longer a condition with your fate in the hands of others. There is a meaning and purpose totally unknown in the world of thought. There is no past and no future. Some of the individuals you now meet were known to your old psyche. They are now almost strangers, and with very strange behaviour patterns. You do not feel superior to them as the concept of comparison does not exist in reality.

You blend in with this strange confused society. It is either that or become a hermit. You will walk along a busy street and look in amazement at an army of sleepwalkers with dead eyes. There is an impulse to tell them about their condition but you don't interfere as you know they would react in the only way they have been led to believe they can. You watch this army of the marching dead as they scurry about, eager to fulfil the whims of their hidden masters. You will have knowledge of the structure and application of magic but will not abuse this ability as you are well aware of the consequences. There will be other abilities which you can use. You will be witness to many more things which cannot be described in any language. This is a very rough outline of the waking process.

THE THOUGHT-MACHINE AND HOW IT FUNCTIONS THROUGH STEALTH

- Target chosen population.
- Infiltrate.
- Attain positions of influence.
- Create false education systems.
- Kill off all original or existing sources of inherited knowledge by driving a wedge between wise elders and vulnerable young.
- Create governmental hierarchies.
- Confuse young minds through lies and trauma.
- Confused young become confused adults.
- Confusion is easily manipulated.
- Create self-perpetuating belief systems which police themselves through fear.
- A constant diet of contradictory lies and nonsense ensures the establishment and maintenance of self-perpetuating confusion.
- Constant confusion of the psyche causes it to become disorientated, thus creating the condition of morbidity.
- Morbidity creates the condition of fear.

The use of fear becomes the key factor in control and manipulation. Permanently installed think-tanks ensure the maintenance of all the above.

The mind caught up in all this nonsense still has the ability to free itself through a system based on pure logical deduction. (*See* Logic). The object of the system is to liberate individuals by helping them to master their mechanical nature and replace unconscious reaction with conscious action. It involves studying the negative aspects of your life, controlling them and strengthening those positive aspects now ignored by the psyche. Those real quality impulses and abilities such as alertness, compassion, serenity, humility and self-discipline are at present drowned out by the diversions of the relentless daily grind created to serve the perverted whims of unseen masters.

Your life is ruled by fear in its many guises and this is why you need to dig deep to find and expose the roots of fear to the light of reason. (*See Fear*). This condition of fear prevents you from freeing yourself from the herd mentality which frowns on anything other than total conformity.

THE SYSTEM

At present your psyche is functioning on automatic pilot. Begin simply by looking at your habits in order to observe their mechanical nature. Here is an exercise in self-remembering. One of the most common habits is scratching an itch. The next time you scratch try to remember to catch yourself in the act. Keep trying. Try to intervene between the itch and the scratch. If you succeed in this, pause for a second or two before scratching. Then deliberately scratch. Something new has happened. You have changed the usual unconscious reactionary habit into a conscious action. You have taken the first step on a journey of self-discovery. If you continue, it will lead to full consciousness. A small beginning, you may think, but it is just the beginning of an effect which will snowball and change your life forever.

The next time you feel an itch, try to stop yourself from scratching it altogether. It may subside or it may become so chronic, a battle of wills ensues between the automatic reactions and your attempt at self-discipline. This shows the schizophrenic nature of the psyche. Repeat this till you feel in control. This exercise develops alertness and self-discipline which you will need in abundance for the more advanced exercises. Not one second is ever wasted in the study of the self. As with any art or craft, the original deep-seated interest and steadfast intention will be the driving force. Try the above with any habit.

Be positive. You can accomplish anything. You just haven't realised it yet. As you look at different habits you will see the different natures of the battles of will which ensue. Your willpower becomes stronger as you progress. Next turn your attention to your relationship with the world around you.

YOUR PLACE IN THE MACHINE

Your psyche is a link in a chain of predictable events. The link before you is everything which impacts on your senses. Your link, which is your psyche, automatically responds to these stimuli, thus giving continuity to a predetermined flow of events. The link after you is the automatic response of another individual to your behaviour. In this way the flow of events continues down the chain from link to link. The functioning of the whole machine relies completely on this predictable behaviour. The whole purpose of conditioning and indoctrination from an early age is to create and maintain this automatic pattern of behaviour. Every psyche on the planet is a link in their local chain, keeping local events easily controlled. In this way every link is contributing to its own enslavement.

Your psyche has many inbuilt triggers which activate certain emotional responses to incoming stimuli. You cannot just sit down and look at these triggers, you wouldn't know where to begin. You have to wait for a situation to arise which activates one of them. With your increased alertness you stand a better chance of self-remembering in this event. Every trigger recalls a particular memory and associated emotion as a result of a previous experience in a similar situation. Before you have a chance to rationalise a situation your psyche has already been thrust into response mode and it is too late, sometimes with dire consequences. Your psyche sees a trigger in the incoming stimuli, when in fact there is no trigger in external stimuli. The trigger is in your own psyche, wound up in defence mode and ready to strike out, as it is caught up in the turmoil of the world of thought.

You reside deep within the psyche, in your comfort-zone, an oasis in the battlefield of the psyche which is the property of the thought-machine and those who control it. You have surrounded your oasis with a defence shield which acts as a sensor, blocking out any data it considers traumatic or a threat to the comfort of the frightened inhabitant of the oasis. So what you imagine to be your defence shield is in fact your jailer, keeping you in perpetual fear of the unknown, the condition of morbidity. The comfort-zone only receives distorted images, as all data is censored as it passes through the surrounding shield. By retreating to the comfort-zone you have effectively cut yourself off from the outside world and direct perception of incoming data. You have nothing to work with except the distorted data sent by the machine via the shield. You are trapped in the morbid condition.

All the above is absolutely true, but whatever you do, don't believe it. Instead, check it out. Investigate it for yourself. Don't take anyone else's word for it. Make the knowledge your own. So how do you stop all this automation which is so mischievous in the world around you and makes a nonsense of your life and the lives of others? The shield is made up of thoughts which have been introduced by an extremely sophisticated system of misinformation into your unsuspecting psyche from birth. A very good experiment which shows up the invasive nature of those thoughts is the counting exercise. This develops attention and concentration.

In bed at night, before you become too drowsy, try counting to a hundred. Take a few deep breaths, then relax and continue breathing normally. Count your breaths in your mind as you exhale. Visualise the numbers in front of you to the exclusion of all else. This exercise has three possible scenarios.

- 1—You will just drift off to sleep
- 2—You will suddenly realise you have lost concentration, cannot

- 3—As you count, you are aware of the numbers but also become aware of another phenomenon. You sense thoughts and even voices attempting to crowd out your concentration. You are fully aware that these thoughts are not your own and were not invited. You can see clearly the invasive nature of these, and even capture what the thoughts were or what the voices said. Very often it does not make sense. Try this and see for yourself.

The thoughts and voices you detected are in fact there all the time. The only reason you were able to detect them was because of your attempt to focus your concentration on one image to the exclusion of all else. You were able to detect them on the periphery of your awareness just as you can be aware of something at the corner of your eye. Usually you are not that focused and fail to notice how the psyche is a playground for these thought-monkeys which are effectively drowning out and incapacitating your finer perceptions. Repeat this till you are satisfied with the results.

All data entering through the physical senses is instantly interpreted within the mechanism of the psyche. By cutting yourself off you have become the terminus at the end of the line of information. By the time you get the information it has already been distorted, giving you a false picture of events in reality. You all too eagerly accept this as a fact. But you are not in possession of the facts and your reactionary behaviour sends out the message that this is your attitude. This attitude is a false one which has overridden your true feelings. Hence there is a distorted communication. As long as you remain locked away in your comfort-zone you will never know what's going on in the outside world. In order to learn anything you must find the courage to step outside the zone. Until you do this you will remain a pawn in someone else's game. So how do you gain control over all this automation?

One of the most common everyday emotions is annoyance. The society you function in is geared to evoke this automatic response many times a day. It could be anything, bad weather, a bad driver, a late bus, or a queue-jumper. Next time, try to catch yourself in this condition of annoyance. Look for the logic in it. You won't find any because there isn't any. It is completely illogical to be annoyed at anything. All it does is burn up your precious energy. Think back and try to remember some occasion when you were annoyed. What did it accomplish? How would things have worked out if you had kept a cool head? To begin with, you would have saved that vital energy, and you would have seen more clearly the situation as it was.

Start by looking at the condition and seeing the futility and foolishness of it. Try controlling it. Don't allow yourself to keep carrying this illogical baggage round with you all the time. As you look at emotions your willpower becomes stronger. Your life begins to change for the better. Every time you control an emotion you store a quantity of energy. There will be a positive effect, not just on you but every other life you touch, every other link in your chain. There are many emotions built into your psyche. Annoyance is one of the mildest. Some are more harmful. Some are highly dangerous. (*See* Emotions).

Your false identity is not the identity you imagine it to be. The psyche is schizophrenic, totally fragmented. The psyche consists of hundreds of totally separate identities. Every thought has it's own individual identity. You are many identities every day of your life. When you experience an emotion it assumes the dominant role over the rest of the psyche. You don't just 'feel' annoyed. You actually become that condition of annoyance. It dictates your behaviour. Either you control it or it controls you. Whatever the emotion, that is your temporary identity, your false reality. The more powerful the emotion, the more it dominates the psyche to the detriment of any finer feelings.

One moment you are enjoying a pleasant day. This calm pleasant condition within your psyche colours your day and you see everything through rose coloured glasses. Life is a joy. Then suddenly some incident occurs and a trigger in your psyche conjures up this condition of annoyance. Now you are a different personality. You can switch identities just like that. The scowling demon of annoyance pushes that happy-go-lucky you to one side and assumes the authority to shout and stamp its feet at some imagined external trigger. Gone are the rose coloured glasses.

These switches occur several times a day. You are never in control, and wear these conditions like a suit of armour. They weigh you down, wear you out and sap all your vital energy, rendering you a mere shadow of what you could be and should be. But you can take charge of the flow of events in your particular chain by altering your behaviour. Self-discipline is the key.

It's raining, so what? Someone tries to annoy you, so what? It is their problem, not yours. The bus is late, so what? Buses are late all the time. Just use the extra waiting time to think of something more constructive. Why burn off all your energy cursing a system of transport which is no more than a joke, not even aware of your existence and barely aware of its own. What people do not know is that your energy-level does not have a fixed level. It is constantly coming into your consciousness, and if stored, it builds up and up. Your energy-level only appears constant because you are always burning it off through emotions. Nobody in this weird society tells you about this sacred energy because they don't know about it themselves.

All emotions are negative. What you may regard as good or positive emotions are in fact not emotions. They are impulses from your true being. As you slowly take control of your life you will begin to notice the lack of

Reawakening to Full Consciousness

discipline in others. The system of discipline applies to all emotions. They range in power from mild annoyance to boiling rage. They are all controllable. Nobody else is aware of your inner journey. It is strictly between you and you. Others may think in their mechanical way that you are a very cool customer, or just plain weird but that is their problem, not yours. On occasion you may feign annoyance just to fit into a particular situation without causing too much friction. This is harmless. As you discipline emotions the gap between your world and that of others will increase. You will feel yourself drifting apart from the chaos around you. Your psyche will fight to keep you in the zone. It will constantly come up with reasons why you should lose your temper, or feel envious or whatever.

Self-remembering helps. In moments of relaxation you will begin to have flashes of awareness of phenomena you never knew existed. You will find it heavy going and want to throw in the towel as you feel your hold on your mind slipping. There will be times when you become disorientated. These occur because you are separating yourself from the old emotional world of thought and you sorely miss the petty little distractions you once cherished. The psyche is losing it's balance without these familiar crutches. You are denying its cravings. This is self-discipline in action.

One of the roles of self-remembering will be to periodically reaffirm your original intention and determination, the act of reaffirmation. Remember, this is a psychological trap and you are seeking full consciousness. There comes a point, the bridge between the illusion and real reality, where you become disorientated as you shed the old beliefs and misconceptions. It will not be a new way of thinking, but the rejection of the thought-process entirely. This will be the ultimate test of sincerity. As you leave the illusion your centre of balance has to make the decision to reject all thought, and then the ultimate decision to withdraw totally from that last bastion, the ego, the sense of a self which imagines itself to be a unit of consciousness inherently separate from other units of consciousness. Only when all concepts have been destroyed is there the possibility of observing reality, that which cannot be destroyed, the ultimate simplicity, that which is. Thinking attempts to fragment the unity of absolute truth. Only when the last candle has been extinguished can you detect the first faint light of dawn.

Your jumping-off point for the final cleansing of the mind will be within the illusion but through work on the psyche, seeing it for what it really is, you have satisfied your higher being that leaving the illusion is the right thing to do, the only thing to do. It is easier these days to explain the concept of illusion as many individuals are now more familiar with the concept of virtual reality. The psyche is easily fooled as it has accepted as definitive reality a combination of learned lies masquerading as truths and apparently corroborative messages from the physical senses. They can see clearly how the clever use of mechanical and electrical manipulation can be made to trick the senses. It is only one step further to explore the possibility of a deeper and more sinister level of trickery, and the validity of what you have always accepted as definitive reality.

None of this is based on hearsay or theory. It is a simple fact. Even though you have had glimpses of real reality you are still a psyche and as such are still vulnerable to attack from within the thought-machine. You are still functioning in a world governed by misguided psyches, not to mention the controllers and their groomed vassals. This is where yoga enters the picture. There is a form of yoga which enables you to split your awareness into two separate aspects. These are mind and psyche, one foot in each camp so to speak. You are not quite ready to pull out of the psyche yet, the last leg of the caterpillar to leave the branch. The world of the psyche is now showing its true colours as a dream.

Can you imagine waking up in the morning and having the ability to carry on in the dream simultaneously with your working life? This is the discipline of yoga. Through this yoga you can maintain a modicum of communication with the psyches around you while at the same time working in isolation to prepare for the coming transition. Alertness and discipline are now a permanent aspect of your life. This will greatly ease the final condition of disorientation when you withdraw from the world of thought. The psyche cannot attack a clear mind as it cannot know the concept of a mind without thought. The clear mind is not subject to the temporal laws of the thought-machine. However, the psyche can attack itself, using thought-weapons such as doubt, guilt, temptation etc, in order to prevent the loss of a link in the chain of events as it is conditioned to do.

Study your psyche with total sincerity. Look for your faults. Examine them one at a time and discipline them. Remember you are seeking an unnameable truth. You have no agenda whatsoever. You do not feel superior to those around you as they are now just as you were at some point in your journey through the world of thought. Question your motives in everything you think and do. Question your reason for seeking truth. Is it your version of truth or are you just seeking a way out of this mess? If your motives are not totally selfless you will get no nearer the real truth.

THE TRANSITION

The final transition will not be a gradual affair. There will be a crisis point, the final rejection of all thought. What lies behind the veil? Is it so great as to justify all this discipline? The answer is a simple yes, but this yes has more meaning than any yes you have ever dreamed of. It is more important than any importance you have ever dreamed of. You cannot compare the dark morbid brutal enslavement of the psyche with the total freedom and beauty of the free mind. Rejecting the psyche breaks the spell of the dream as you are leaving every concept of time. (*See* Time).

It is not that you leave time and go outside it to some mysterious realm. All time just ceases to exist. You can plainly see how time was just a dream-concept and never did exist. The concepts of past and future dissolve into nothingness. Just the present remains. This immeasurable present is just an ever-changing moment, there is no imagined future laden with false promises and no past to overshadow the present living moment of psychological freedom. The moment is ever new, the beginning and end all in one. Everything is done for the right reasons, and not because of the morbid demanding of a spent moment of present or the instilled fear of some imagined future consequences.

When you see through the concept of past and future you don't 'go' anywhere. You remain where you always were, here and now. Here is the only place you will ever be and now is the only time you will ever be here. As your mind clears there are ever fewer thoughts remaining, ever fewer concepts. You are well aware that none of these represent the ultimate truth. A point will come when you are ready to dispel the last of them. You may be lying in bed, walking or just relaxing in a chair. You will know when the moment arrives.

Up to now you have been residing in your comfort-zone, a private dream you have created to protect your sense of self from the chaos of the greater dream around you. When you have killed off the last thoughts there still remains that which killed them off, you. You are aware in your higher being that this entity cannot be trusted any more than the thoughts it just killed off. The only answer is psychological suicide. The ultimate act of transforming arrogance into humility demands no courage as the enormity of the importance of what you have witnessed on your journey renders the concept of self meaningless and propels your awareness from the dream into the reality of absolute truth.

If you walk along the wrong road for two miles, suddenly realise your mistake, stop and turn round, you still face the undoing of the mistake. This will be the two-mile walk back. When the psyche creates a concept the opposite concept comes into being. You think comfort and the possibility of discomfort is created. You imagine you have just created the concept of comfort but you have created the two-sided coin of comfort-discomfort. So by imagining you are living in the side of comfort you are in effect denying the side of discomfort. You end the denial by facing the other side of the coin which you have created. You created it from nothing and held the two halves apart. Now you are allowing them to come back together and dissolve back into nothingness. In that nothingness is truth, that which simultaneously is, was and always will be.

When you sacrifice the condition of comfort the self faces extreme discomfort, and finds this unbearable. It begs to be allowed back into the world of thought and all its foolish little distractions, but nobody and nothing hears and it is left in a limbo so terrible it defies description. But it is for the sake of truth and all will be well. Only total humility can enter reality.

LIMBO
Just an infinitesimal spark of the old self remains as it is withdrawn from the comfort-zone. It is now suspended in a void of nothingness. The void is so profound that even the void does not exist. The word profound is totally inadequate. This limbo is the final condition of the self where the last trace of false identity is burned off. It is not a physical burning but a mental one. You thought it was you but it wasn't. You are about to find out what the real you is.

You think you have jumped off a cliff and may be dashed to pieces on the rocks below but you are not capable of caring as there is no longer a you to care, it is now dying. But that which cannot be destroyed has survived the cessation of thought and is aware of the void. It knows also that the rocks, the cliff and all the rest were just part of the illusion, the last throw of the dice by the dying dream. There is a total loss of memory in a terrible mental wipe-out. A tiny spark of awareness drifts in the void. It knows nothing but quietly observes the abysmal blackness. There is a total absence of any concept to relate to, just an unbearable emptiness.

In this utterly indescribable condition the last shred of self withers away. Along with the self, the last trace of the concept of guilt also disappears. Guilt is the vague awareness of the possibility of a reoccurrence of that which has been seen to be a negative reaction. (*See* Guilt). Your body sits in the chair. It has literally lost its mind but there is an unnameable something looking through the eyes and it sees a strange place. It is a helpless infant in a stranger's body. Over the years, individuals who have studied the psyche have lived in isolated communities or esoteric schools because of the debilitating nature of disorientation.

The individual becomes like a child again. The condition can last for days, weeks or even years, depending on how deeply the individual was involved in the dream of the psyche. During this period the helpless individual is cared for till the condition slowly wears off and the fog lifts to reveal the dawn of consciousness, a sunrise, the beauty of which can never be imagined. Some of those who have attempted these studies in the outside world have ended up in lunatic asylums as the condition of disorientation is not understood by the psyches in charge. There has always been a knowledge of esoteric activity by the demonic controllers of earth who sought out and murdered those students of truth, as they are seen as a serious threat to the prevailing system of corruption.

This new intelligence can make the body move and stand up.

Movement is clumsy. Speaking is difficult as there is limited memory of language. Everything is for the first time. Your hand touches a surface to feel the sensation. You cannot relate to anything or anyone. You fish for memories but nothing bites. There is a gentle dawning that this is your real identity. It is not an individual identity with a sense of self but a true universal un-fragmented identity, a union with the all-pervading intelligence of that which is.

You are now aware of a profound silence. Not a physical silence but a mental one. You realise the silence is the absence of the chattering monkeys of learned thought and concepts which used to jump about arguing with each other and creating conflict in the psyche by attaching emotions to your pure memories. The noise used to drown out the silence but now the silence drowns out the loudest noise. Your ears can still hear physical noise but none of it bothers you as there is no psychological or emotional reaction to it. Everything is accepted without resistance or complaint.

There is just pure observation. Some memories begin to return, but in a pure form having been cleansed of all connotations. As these memories return you are still in the void and still cannot relate to the world around you. Things seem somehow distant as though you are looking at society through the wrong end of a telescope. You feel you have just arrived from another universe. You improvise and do whatever it takes to fit in and establish a modicum of communication by simulating the behaviour and speech of these strange confused people. You no longer try to do anything. You simply do it. The question never arises whether you can do it or not. Everything is effortless. There is enormous energy. This is super-thought. (*See* Super-thought).

Your memory of language returns. There is still the void so you use yoga to get by. You see society for what it is, a vast lunatic asylum where the sane ones are regarded as mad and the mad ones are worshipped by fools. It is a society so full of unnecessary problems they are overlapping. People known to your old psyche seem very odd. You do not judge them as the concept of judgment does not exist in real reality. You just observe them in their confusion, doing the will of their hidden masters. You help them when they allow it. You only tell them the truth if they ask specifically. You are now truly an actor on a stage while the condition of disorientation lasts. It will gradually ease and the fog will clear.

It is important to establish the difference between the words 'finite' and 'infinite'. Many use the word infinity without really understanding what it means. Everything in the world of thought is finite, or limited to a specific measurement. No matter how many times you multiply a given measurement it is always finite and relative to a bigger one. There is always that extra inch. (*See* Time, Space and Motion). The psyche cannot ever conceive of infinity as the real meaning is beyond the conceptual. The psyche can only grasp that which has a beginning and end. Infinity has no beginning or end. Only the unimaginable and unnameable is infinite. The meaning of infinity cannot be communicated to the psyche except through the medium of Kundalini. (*See* Kundalini).

You will never understand infinity till you leave time. You now marvel at the many wonders around you which others cannot see. You do not feel superior as there are no emotions. If there were emotions there would be no pure observations. You know that this is it. There is nowhere left to go. This is the final resting place. There is the awareness that all those trapped in psyches and suffering will at a certain point be joining the ranks of the free. You become aware of certain abilities, not powers, as the concept of power belongs only in the world of thought.

You experiment with these abilities to determine their nature, but not to harm or take advantage of others. Once you have established the authenticity of an ability you never use it again. You need nothing. You want nothing. You have everything. You are everything and everyone. Your heart is as light as a feather and is filled with the light of a million suns. You have the use of Kundalini. Your vibrations have become incredibly fine. It feels like a singing sensation in your head. What feels like liquid electricity flows up your spine and fills your head. The sensation is indescribable.

KUNDALINI

The vibrations become finer giving a higher note. The note is not physically audible. It is sensed in the mind.

As the note rises it acquires an indefinable sweetness. This sweetness is not that of sugar or the scent of flowers but the sweetness of a beauty which transcends the physical senses. It is purely spiritual. It increases in intensity as it rises with the vibrations. It is accompanied by an increasingly ecstatic feeling of extreme well-being.

The sweetness is felt at the base of the spine, the whole spine and the brain. It emanates from the base of the spine and through the brain.

There is a sensation of physical faintness due to the overwhelming beauty of the sweetness. The vibrations continue to become finer till they reach vanishing point. There is now a silence filled with the indescribable beauty of the collective consciousness.

You are infinitely beyond all knowledge.

You are in heaven.

The force spreads around you. You feel as light as a feather. People and animals in your vicinity can feel this sensation. Animals come to be near you to bathe in these vibrations. They seem to be more aware than people.

They are aware that you are at the centre of this phenomenon and they look at you in wonderment, at this feeling they never knew before. This feeling is exquisite beyond description.

People feel the sensations but are not aware of the source. It can affect a whole crowd. As you enter their vicinity they become aware of an indefinable but exquisite feeling of ecstasy. It sweeps over them and within seconds they are all chattering happily as though stoned out of their heads. The reason for this is because they are suddenly in the moment when the effects of Kundalini have temporarily wiped out all negative thoughts. Their concepts of past and future have been suspended. The spirit of truth can penetrate anywhere through the medium of Kundalini.

Whenever you feel this sensation of Kundalini mysterious things occur. If you walk into an empty shop it soon fills with customers. You are so alert you can detect a flash of lightning an instant before it materialises. You have the ability to spiritually meld with another individual. You can detect a fleeting red glow in the eyes of those who are possessed or influenced by demons. You can sense the hideous otherworldly mental smell of a demon when they come near. (*See* Demons).

Any concept or sensation can be sent into any psyche through Kundalini. It is only proper to use Kundalini to help others. There is also a knowledge of magic, how and why it works. This magic can be understood and used by any psyche but this knowledge you do not divulge. By sacrificing the false identity you have freed a link from the chain. You cannot lose any more as you have left the casino, the rat-race. From reality you can see and understand the illusion. The illusion, on the other hand is totally unaware of reality. You have made the final transition from non-existence to existence. You have awakened from a dream that never was. You have attained lucidity in the first and last stirring of full consciousness.

Real Values

The psyche fears the possibility of its own extinction. This extinction is inevitable either intentionally or unintentionally. In a life where the awakening process has begun, the true identity begins to re-establish itself and discipline the psyche. The seed of truth is germinating in such a psyche. It begins to discern a new importance as opposed to a transitory string of unexplained whims. Extraordinary insights are revealed. A message to those who fear the passing into oblivion of all those values they hold dear, be they beautiful moments they have known or the very existence of a real tangible goodness in the physical world. Things of real value never pass away. They are indestructible. Every real value you have ever known is yours in eternity. Those values will be with you to help as you go back through the gateway of time itself.

Relics

Relics have real effect as they have been saturated by extremely powerful vibrations. They are truly sacred as they have seen absolute consciousness. Everything, animate or inanimate has a level of consciousness and memory.

Religion

Religion is and always was hand in hand with established governments as a means of curtailing true human endeavour. The mind had to be converted to a psyche first as a free mind cannot be controlled. (*See* Psyche). Religion is a cunning concept as it functions on fear and is self- perpetuating. Many brave individuals who feared nothing in life were suddenly filled with fear at the prospect of some unknown terror after death.

Religion is a disease injected into the psyche's capacity for blind belief. Religion consists of a great many falsehoods with the occasional truth thrown in to give it an apparent respectability and to woo the doubtful psyche. Religion lauds as it's heroes worthy individuals who in reality had no time whatsoever for the poppycock of organised religions whose peddlers of poison wore fancy dress costumes, lived in mansions, built palatial cathedrals and collected money from those who already lived in poverty. That's enough about religion.

Science

The whole of the so-called official scientific establishment is there to do the bidding of the elite. One of its functions has been to maintain the primitive level of human society. It is a conspiracy of epic proportions, a stage performance on a grand scale. Whenever an independent thinker cried eureka the machinery sprang into action to assess the threat to the establishment agenda. If it was a genuine discovery it was immediately purchased and totally suppressed. There is nothing which has not already been discovered or invented eons before the first human seed graced the planet earth.

As humanity evolved and began to discover natural interactions between certain phenomena the controllers of earth sneered, having long suppressed all such knowledge. The whole object of the establishment of official science was to suppress all independent human progress and keep all knowledge in the hands of the few elite till it is time to step in and take complete control of the lives of humanity. Apart from those in the know at the top of this pyramid of deception there are the hordes of foolish little white-coated monkeys sincere in the belief that they can ever learn anything from all this crass nonsense. While feeding themselves this line they are busy chasing the material merits attached to the swish of the white coats. A complete and utter sham. All so-called new discoveries are no more than selectively leaked drips from the reservoir of knowledge.

In a desperate attempt to keep control of the public psyche those who have for so long been manipulating human affairs are now mixing in blind religious beliefs with their phony concocted theories, a sop to the zealots.

A trapped rat will chew its own leg off.

The idea behind this move is to give the impression that these beliefs are really just an integral part of the overall process of their famous scientific theories. (Which have been changing more frequently than the weather over hundreds of years). All theories are in essence an attempt to justify the denial of the existence of the souls of humanity. Their think-tanks are constantly overhauling their psychological trickery.

They have been watching from the shelter of the shadows. Now the shadows are gone and the watchers are being watched in their self-created prison like monkeys in a cage.

They refer to the psyche as the soul. Such a statement is utterly ridiculous. The psyche is merely an individual bundle of thoughts, simply a wheel within the thought machine.

The actual soul is the real inner being, the very essence of the individual life force which is totally free in every way and can never be subject to nonsensical worthless theories which totally alienate themselves from facts.

Self-remembering

Self-remembering is the affirmation of a discipline or conscious decision. What you are remembering is the true self, and not some automatic chain of whims, the origin of which are independent and alien to the individual life force. There is the sense of real self which is consciousness. There is the sense of self-importance which is no more than an aspect of the self- deceptive psyche.

Sexuality and Sex

There is no subject about which there is more confusion than sexuality. Sexuality and the physical act of sex are separate issues. Sexuality is a spiritual state. Sex is a physical function. The combination of both is the fulfilment of humanity. Male and female are the opposite sides of the coin of sexuality. The union of the two halves is the sacred expression and celebration of the beauty of creation, the total fulfilment of consciousness. There are those who are fully male or female. There are those who are confused. The more powerful the magnet the greater the attraction. Male is positive and female is negative in an electrical sense. This does not mean one is better than the other. Both are exactly equal in their collective contribution to life as components of a potentially single unit.

In order to confuse young vulnerable individuals there are those who put into circulation the false idea that there is really very little difference between male and female. Nothing is further from the truth. Nothing in creation could be more different. This difference is the sacred basis of all creation. To deny this is to deny truth itself. Homosexuality is an aberration from the natural flow of life which can have several causes. It can be hereditary influence. It can be a karmic issue where the individual was an abuser of the opposite sex in a previous existence. It can be the result of confusing and misleading education or it can be the result of interference by a paedophile. It is totally wrong to condemn homosexuals as they cannot help what they are. Allowances must be made for them. (*See* Masculinity and Femininity).

Although there are genuine homosexuals, there are also many confused individuals not to mention those who aggravate the situation for their own agendas. As long as homosexuals do not encroach on your way of life, you have no right to condemn them. There are far more important issues other than homosexuality waiting for your attention.

Either sex may remain alone but this in no way detracts from their sexual potency. The magnetism is still there. A male who dislikes females is not a complete male and vice versa. Every psyche lives in its own world but may share their world with another individual with genuine commitment. A male does not have a feminine side, as some would have you believe. A real male is kind, gentle and tender with females. There is nothing feminine about that. It is just how a male should be, not a brutal, belligerent psychopath who is disrespectful of females. A real male has nothing to prove and has no complexes about sexuality. On the other hand, a brutal or arrogant male lacks masculinity and feels there is something to prove. True human beings have total respect for the opposite sex.

The original deniers of truth have created hybrids of themselves to ensure compliance and cooperation from the caretakers. These hybrids or non-humans substitute physical sex alone in place of meaningful sexual relationships. They are totally unaware of the sanctity of a true union between male and female and therefore totally lack any form of respect or true appreciation of the opposite sex.

When the sexes meet they give of their essence to each other via psychic and electrical forces. This does not require a physical sex act. It can be an extremely spiritual experience. The actual sex act is the final union in order to create new life. If the creation of new life is not yet desired there are provisions for that these days besides, there are many ways to indulge in sex without actual penetration. In a completely spiritual relationship just being close to a particular member of the opposite sex is pure ecstasy and infinitely superior to any casual physical sex. In human relationships the atmospherics are more important than the mechanics.

Due to perverted religious preaching, with the intention of creating a false sense of guilt masturbation is a harmful act and sin. In fact nothing is more natural. The same goes for eroticism. It is of the utmost importance in any truly civilised society. A strip-show is a welcome break from the cares of the day and relieves stress. The physical sex act is used in so-called black magic ceremonies. There are magical procedures which use the orgasm in conjunction with certain mental conditions to attain a goal. There are ceremonies where the female is drugged and raped, even murdered. In these cases, usually in the pursuit of political ends, the orgasm is used in conjunction with certain coded words and a highly trained will power and visualisation of the desired agenda. The killing of the victim is a sacrificial offering to appease the particular astral demon involved and is carried out in the most painful way possible. This ceremony emits incredibly powerful vibrations and usually has the desired results. Of course it goes without saying that if you indulge in anything of that nature it would be a wiser alternative to throw yourself under an express train.

There are other non-ceremonial methods whereby any male may seduce any desired female but alas this information is not given here for obvious reasons. Sexual energy is the most potent power in the astral or thought-world and is used every day in many ways, often unwittingly. Sexuality is the most sacred and the most abused aspect of earthly life. No psyche would be able to cope with the knowledge of the astronomical amount of suffering and karmic build-up caused by this. There is almost no place on earth where this state of affairs is honestly dealt with as the lily-livered individuals in positions of influence are incapable of disciplining their lustful cravings.

Apart from the main meal of human suffering, astral demons consume loveless, lustful and violent sexual vibrations for dessert. Puberty is the beginning of the sex life of the individual. The physical changes coincide with psychic and the innermost spiritual development. The spirit has temporary responsibility for a physical body. Promiscuity is the result of confusion, morbidity and peer pressure. All promiscuity leads the individual down the road of karma as all casual sex passes down the chain of cause and effect in which each individual is ultimately accountable.

Creation is a circular spherical movement, coming from and returning to the source of truth. It is a combination of existence and non-existence. The ultimate truth, or existence is unknowable as it is beyond thought. Non-existence, or the creation of movement is knowable as the concept of

Sexuality & Sex

thought is within the creation of all possibilities. Every knowable aspect of this creation is composed of two opposites. The free will has the ability to know and experience the essence of any half of any aspect. Both halves of all aspects remain related due to the pull of the original separation. The point at which the two halves re-join is the reunion with existence and full consciousness.

Everything in creation is a male or a female half of a created aspect. So it is with human sexuality. Most human coupling is non-spiritual, therefore the two halves remain separate, each continuing in their own illusory world. Their sexual activity lacks spiritual union at the moment of orgasm. Drugs are used in the misguided belief that it greatly enhances the pleasure of sex and makes it a spiritual experience. This is not true. No drug ever caused a spiritual experience. The psyche, which is unaware of the conscious mind has steeped itself in the physical world and accepts it as the only reality becomes a part of that world and is subject to all the consequences of its beliefs. Drugs only affect the physical brain and jumble up the vibrations normally interpreted through the senses.

The drugged psyche interprets colours as sounds and sees sounds and so forth. The individual is born with the natural wherewithal to develop spiritually. Drugs become a crutch and an escape from boredom thus destroying the natural flow of normal development. Drugs are just another circus trick and nothing remotely to do with spiritually attained happiness.

The sex act is the nearest the psyche can come to spontaneity. It is the only activity where it can give its full attention without the interference of other considerations. It is the ultimate escape while it lasts but as soon as it has ended it's back to square one, and as with any other temporal excitement or craving it becomes a meaningless obsession with many square ones and all the old inner conflicts returning. Proper education is badly needed. With the development of Kundalini it is possible to meld or become one with any member of the opposite sex. With an intimate knowledge of vibrations and the aura it is possible to momentarily stop the outflow of one's own aura or essence creating a vacuum which sucks in the essence of the individual concerned.

This is how it functions. Because of the mental noise and inner conflict of your everyday psyche all your interpreted projections are outgoing. This is creating a one-way traffic system leaving no room for the incoming traffic of the signals and essence of others. You are effectively isolating yourself. Just as yoga can slow down and stop breathing and heartbeats the aura can be temporarily neutralised, creating inner silence. You are immediately filled with the essence of the other individual. This is known as melding.

The result is an extraordinary powerful flow of electricity between the two. The closer the two the stronger the flow. It can be physically felt as a liquid electrical pulsing. It is a complete consummation of body, mind and spirit. The individual you meld with is instantly aware of this and if there is eye-contact there is an explosion of physically visible pure white light reminiscent of a powerful camera flash. Both minds become one for an instant. The physical effects are overpowering. The burst of light completely fills both your minds and hearts. It is the ultimate intimacy with the opposite sex. You are both united in the instant single throb of a shared heartbeat. The whole occurs in an instant but can never be forgotten. One such moment justifies your whole existence.

To force yourself on a member of the opposite sex is the thin end of the wedge of rape. There should be total unconditional respect and a relationship should be approached with care. To force yourself on another is disrespectful and by doing so you forfeit your right to a reciprocal respect. The orgasm has the most sacred place in the act of physical sex. As a general rule this is hopelessly misunderstood. The orgasm is the peak of planetary life. All life has one end, the complete union of the male and female aspects. The actual function of the orgasm is the complete saturation of minds and bodies by the power of the spirit. It has a profound effect on the new life created. All astral demons are paedophiles by nature. Demons have a vastly more developed intellect than the human psyche. To them, all humans are vulnerable children. They prey on children and adults alike. A human adult is a two-year-old in their eyes. (*See* Demons). Their one aim is to sexually destroy humanity.

Circumcision is the cowardly act of child mutilation. Contrary to the waffle of forced belief systems this is a heinous crime against innocent defenceless children. It is perpetrated on false pretexts. This primitive custom actually destroys the sensitivity of sex organs and many children have died in agony from infections in unhygienic conditions. In male-dominated societies females are abused in this fashion to remove the natural female pleasure from the sex act and reduce them to subservient child-bearers. In the male, the foreskin is the natural covering to protect and maintain the sensitivity of the head of the penis. In the female, the labia majora serves the same purpose. In the primitive circumcision of females the labia majora and the clitoris are literally hacked off with sharp stones, causing many deaths. There is nothing more ignorant and uncivilised on earth. And so the ignorance continues until such time when human beings begin to think for themselves. Those who have never known a truly spiritual relationship with the opposite sex will at some point know it and only then will they know the meaning of life. Your most treasured idea of heaven is agony by comparison. Institutionalised celibacy is a devious invention totally contrary to true nature and provides cover for the activity of paedophiles. It is the sole right of every individual whether or not to remain celibate.

Sincerity

Sincerity is an elusive quality. In true meditation the aim is to by-pass the self-deceptive psyche and reach a point where the content of the mind is totally sincere. This point cannot be reached until the last trace of self-deception is rejected. The psyche must continue to question its own motives. A pure state of humility must be established, leaving no loose ends. Only such a state can be receptive to revelation.

States, Qualities, Conditions, Mind and Psyche

The alert silent mind is a conscious state of being. It is totally free in the truest sense of the word and subject to nothing. The psyche or sleeping mind is an unconscious condition. It is a prisoner of thought and subject to all influences. When a mind gives its fullest attention to the physical dream it's clarity fades imperceptibly and it loses touch with consciousness. It slips into the hypnotic world of clichéd thought, ceases to be a state and becomes a condition in a world already occupied by ancient influences with a non-human agenda.

It is vulnerable as it has temporarily lost touch with the protection of consciousness. All experiences are then conditions thrust upon it by the agenda of the dream. The concept of subjugation is created solely by base, bestial, predatory and totally insane thought-entities or demons. All conditions follow automatically as a result of the belief in, and the acceptance of the concept of subjugation. Conditions include all emotions, miseducation, false concepts and morbidity. The accumulation of these conditions renders the psyche impotent, reducing the vast majority of planetary life to absolute chaos and suffering. On the other hand the wakeful mind can see through all the little tricks of the dream-game which denies the waking state. A state is an aspect of the conscious awareness of ultimate truth. A quality is action born of such a state. Sacred states of mind are, appreciation, awareness, consciousness, ecstasy, femininity, humility, innocence, masculinity, quietism, sensation, serenity. These inner states of mind manifest outwardly as sacred qualities in the world of thought of which the physical is a part. Sacred qualities are, affirmation, alertness, altruism, austerity, compassion, contemplation, dignity, discipline, faith, harmony, honour, humour, logic, introspection, martyrdom, respect, sincerity and vitality. The silent observer makes no demands on anything in creation and is impelled by the saviour of humanity.

Suffering

The concept of suffering as an integral part of life is totally unacceptable. There is a stream of thought running through society suggesting that suffering is a necessary and legitimate part of living. This misconception is maintained in order to psychologically render acceptable that which in truth is utterly unacceptable. It is a necessary part of ultimate control. It lays the groundwork for foisted concepts such as religion, karma, wars, slavery, and disease and above all the strange habit of one individual bowing to the will of another. This is the greatest myth, the myth of authority.

Once you have paid homage to this myth the suffering begins. Obedience is the sacrifice of dignity. You are in truth a free individual answerable to no authority, either that of arrogant individuals or that of the notion of acceptable suffering. (*See* Authority). There are two types of suffering, involuntary or voluntary. Involuntary or automatic suffering, either mental or physical, creates the vibrations which provide exciting food for demons. During the process of involuntary suffering the last drop of individual psychic essence is milked by demons in the form of extremely powerful vibrations. (*See* Demons and Human Suffering). Voluntary suffering is beyond the field of thought, therefore beyond the limited awareness of astral entities which inhabit the world of thought. Demons cannot detect it. It is not automatic, but a fully conscious sacrifice which introduces positivity into a negative situation.

Some will argue that situations constantly arise where suffering is unavoidable. This is a feeble attempt to justify suffering. The answer to such a dumb theory is that such situations in themselves are neither acceptable nor logical to begin with. In the course of everyday sane living isolated cases of incidental suffering could occur but this does not mean that suffering is any kind of natural pattern woven into the fabric of life.

There is absolutely no need for a single human being to go hungry for even a moment. Neither is there any reason why they should lose their lives as a consequence of floods, volcanoes, fire, tsunamis or earthquakes. Large sections of humanity have been forced by stealth to inhabit dangerous areas without adequate dwellings capable of withstanding such catastrophes. The elite nest in safe areas while humanity is scorned and exploited by them in every possible way.

Superthought

The psyche which has worked on itself in order to bypass conventional mechanical thought reaches a point where the cultivation of alertness creates a new mentality. It has negated the automatic process and attained permanent alertness. This new mentality is no longer a condition, but a state of mind. This new phenomenon is Superthought. It functions through logic and is the manifestation of the spirit in the physical world. It is endowed with all the finer qualities of humanity and has the ability to interact fully with the physical while remaining in touch with the spiritual. It is still a mental process but a great many times faster than the normally accepted process, having got rid of the clutter. This is another yogic discipline where it is used in the martial arts where the alertness is developed. (*See* Yoga).

Talent

Talent is a gift given freely, and not intended to be sold on at a profit. It is there to share, not to be exploited by the alien, soulless, self-proclaimed elite.

Time, Space and Motion

From the perspective of the psyche within perceptible creation the ultimate source of all is invisible. You are a prisoner in a virtual reality and denied real education. As a result you find yourself faced with a puzzle, a world in which nothing seems to add up. All avenues leading to true answers have been deliberately blocked-off. Everything consists of energy created by consciousness. Within the sphere of consciousness free will has the ability to manipulate this energy which then manifests in the form of wavelengths forming an apparently physical universe. Many wills have become trapped in mazes of their own making while exploring all possibilities. (*See* Creation and Free Will).

The brain decodes the wavelengths which impact on the four sensors of touch, sight, hearing and taste just as radio, phones and television decode the signals sent by the programme makers. In today's world of virtual reality machines this point is easier to understand. Apart from the data impacting on the physical sensors there is a more refined form of data being fed to the psyche which is an entity of greatly lowered awareness. As a result of this the psyche steps in and interprets the data decoded by the brain, giving a distorted view of the original decoded data. In this way the psyche creates it's own little individual virtual reality world, causing division.

Imagine being blind and deaf without the senses of touch and taste. The impacting data would cease to be decoded and the world around you would cease to exist for you so that only your true identity would remain. Now switch those receivers back on and you are back in virtual reality. The only thing you can trust is your own sincere enquiry in order to find elusive answers.

TIME

The Pendulum and its relation to Gravity, Time, Weight and Measurement

All original times, weights and measurements were derived from the pendulum. These were sacred or natural measurements relating directly to the gravity of the perceptible universe. Non-human influences later introduced false measurements for the purposes of expediency in business dealings
 and the control of humanity's wealth and activities. The pendulum is a simple device. It is just a small weight on a rod or piece of string. Once set in motion it maintains a constant rhythm.

How the Pendulum Functions

The pendulum swings in an arc. The curvature of the arc is determined by the length of the radius. As the initial impetus creates the inertia which carries the weight up in the arc it reaches a point where the pull of gravity equals the thrust of that inertia causing it to stop. Gravity immediately pulls it back down into the arc. At the bottom of the arc the inertia created by gravity takes over and carries the weight to the other side and so on. If a gentle swing is maintained the rhythm remains constant irrespective of the length of the arc. This is because the pull of gravity compensates for any extra impetus by contributing an exact counter-pull to any variation in the length of the arc resulting from that impetus.

If the radius is very short the weight swings more steeply away from gravity so the pull of gravity is stronger thus maintaining a faster rhythm. If the radius is very long the weight swings very little away from gravity thus maintaining a much slower rhythm. If left swinging on its own it eventually comes to a stop. However, it continues to compensate and so maintains a constant rhythm to the end. This was always known and the principle was used to adjust and maintain the rhythm of timing devices where the impetus was supplied by weights, water-power, or springs. The grandfather clock is a prime example. The pendulum is also used in dowsing. There are many good books on the subject of dowsing. There is also information on how times, weights and measurements were derived.

Clock Time

When you look at a clock you think you are looking at time. You are not. You are looking at circular movement marked off in segments. The clock is just a machine created to govern all other machines in today's mechanical society. Hours, minutes and seconds do not exist. They are purely imaginary. The controllers have introduced false measurements to control and milk the workforce which is humanity. Clocks were made in order to drag you out of bed on a dark freezing winter morning to make your way to a place of morbid labour where another clock calls for the treadmill to start turning. It's what your parents did so you think of it as being a normal way to live your life.

The minutes on the clock face are to you what the drumbeats were to the galley slave. The clock reads ten to six. You think, it is ten to six now! You look at it later and it reads five to six. You think, it is five to six now! On both occasions it is now, so where did the five minutes go? Now try looking at the minute hand for five minutes without taking your eyes off it and you will see the continuity of now. You realise there are not two now's but just one continuous beginning without an end. You can see that the five minutes does not, never did and never will exist. You can see there is no division between then and now, as then does not exist. It is purely psychological. Is there a clock on a tree in every forest? How did the world of nature and its inhabitants survive before the advent of the clock? Enough about clocks.

Psychological Time

If you walk from A to B you think of B as being in the future. As you walk you take the present with you. It is now when you set off and when you reach your destination it is still that same now. The same applies to space. When you begin your journey you are here. You imagine your destination to be over there, but when you arrive you are still here. You can never escape from here and now.

You did not exist in some past. You will never exist in some future. You only exist now. You were never over there. You never will be over there. You are always here now. You are not a body. You are a mind which allowed itself to be invaded and taken over by a psyche which interprets as reality the data which is spoon-fed. You say you will do something tomorrow but when you come to do it you find it is still today. Tomorrow has moved forward a day. This business of tomorrow is always out of reach, an imaginary attachment to the front of now.

It's just like the donkey with the carrot on a stick. This proves that the concept of the future is a myth where wishes and promises are kept. When you say you will do something on Monday, Tuesday, or Wednesday you are merely organising now. Have your ever done something tomorrow? Obviously not, and you never will. If you are not happy with the present you are psychologically reaching out for a non-existent future and in doing so you stretch the present experience. The desire to get away fills the present with negativity which magnifies the down side. The concept of the future becomes a fantasy replacement for now. The stronger the desire for the comfort of a supposed future the more you feel the discomfort of the present, creating a drag effect. If you are enjoying the present you are psychologically trying to push away that supposedly less enjoyable future, thus compressing the present experience. The vague awareness of the concept of future is always there either stretching or compressing the present experience. It creates time distortion in the psyche and robs the present of your full attention. The sense of time is not in the movement. It is in the perception of that movement. Action in the present does not affect an imaginary future. It only effects the fulfilment of the present. (*See* Karma)

You are waiting in the rain for a bus. Behind you is a cinema in which the audience is enjoying an exciting film. Your perception of time and theirs are totally different, the perception of time being subject to conditions. Half an hour would feel like two hours to you while it would feel like ten minutes to the audience. That is a ratio of twelve to one. Taken to extremes, the ratio of time perception between an individual undergoing severe torture and one high on drugs could be hundreds to one.

The past is just an echo of a present moment spent,
Just a trick to make you think that's where the present went.
Just a base, an empty space where memories ferment,
Without that stalking shadow there is nothing to resent.
The slate is clean, the new beginning leaves your life content,
Of future, there is nothing, but more weapons to invent.
A concept from the sea of fear and by a demon sent.
To pierce the hearts of those who fear some make-believe event.
With consequences dire and a grief beyond comment,
So come back to the present and proceed with good intent.
There are no hours among the flowers nor minutes to distract.
The bees upon the breeze don't have a watch and that's a fact.
Honey on your breakfast tray with good health to endow.
All you need to do is just enjoy this moment now.
Memories will always linger there,
 jigsaw pieces floating in mid-air.
Some will hurry by and disappear,
Like summer insects buzzing past your ear.
At a distance some will tantalize,
Hiding some illusive long lost prize.
Thought declares that memories be cast,
To a place of shadows they call past.
For all that preachers preach and teachers teach,
Future is a place you'll never reach.
By your death bed waiting at your side,
Returning to the shore upon the tide,
Memories come surfing through the mist,
To let you know that time does not exist.
Freed now from illusions of the past,
That long lost prize of now is yours at last.

Time, Perception and Age

Why does time seem to go faster with age? At any point in your life your psyche consists of the sum total of your accrued experiences. The psyche does not 'have' a memory bank. It 'is' a memory bank, a container in which beliefs, concepts and emotions are converted into memories and stored. These are recalled automatically by various trigger mechanisms. These recordings build up with age and the psyche becomes crowded.

CHILDHOOD
A very young psyche contains very few memories and is still just leaving the stage of clear- mindedness. At a certain point a psyche becomes established due to the force-feeding of false concepts through the medium of thought. At this stage the child does not dwell on the possibility of death. Its future seems to stretch on forever. Its days are full of wonder and it cannot wait for the next day's adventures. Its imagined future is filled with glamorous possibilities. The child's psyche has not yet become a morbid creature with fixed habits.

5 year old's self-image

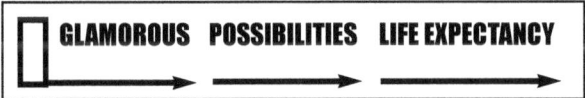

THE MIDDLE YEARS
As the psyche moves through life the development of habitual behaviour causes it to skip through situations previously crammed with interest in the novelty of new experiences. This dilutes the fullness of awareness, psychologically compressing the moment by jumping to the next habit. Life has become a chain of clichés. The psyche is now morbid and set in its ways, a prisoner of the machine. It now sees its expected future as being less than it's past. The hoped-for glamour has been mixed with hardship and disappointment. It takes what it can from the diminishing store of pleasures with one eye on the ever present ghost of a future. It wants to remain fifty but the changing illusion will not allow it. It's perception of time now speeds up.

50 year old's self-image

OLD AGE
The eighty year old psyche thinks it has seen and done it all to the best of its ability. The glamour is quickly fading. There are often such emotions as regret, bitterness, etc. This creates negativity as it faces the approaching prospect of death. It sees death as the ending of what it has been led to believe is its only life and identity. Not wanting the remaining years to slip away makes them appear to slip away even faster. The effect snowballs. The end approaches like an express train slowing down to touch the buffers at the end of the line. Life becomes less physical and more mental. The triggers become more active, awakening memories of the journey. Time becomes a precious commodity like the last piece of cake on the plate. While the psyche is busy with its memories of the fading self the buffers creep closer and it's always a surprise and sometimes a shock when they finally touch. The aged psyche is subject to many ailments. One of these is a condition resembling a second childhood. There comes a point where memories are the only remaining aspect of real value in its life. Certain accumulated memories have a similar effect to time-travel, sending the psyche back to the comfortable years of childhood. (*See* Time-Travel).

80 year-old's self-image

The child has few memories and vastly more future than past. The fifty year old has less future than past.
The eighty year old is choc-a-block with memories and little future. The ratio between accumulated memories and expected future determines time perception.

Time Travel

Every moment has its own unique essence It is the sum total of data recorded by the psyche within the framework of the strongest emotion in that moment. It includes age, sex, health, interests, personal priorities, location, time of day, relationships, tunes, news headlines, books, films, radio and television programmes, work, weather, smells, sensations and the emotion to the fore in that moment. All these aspects together create an identity for that moment. As the months and years pass, the overall condition and essence of the body changes piecemeal. It is the same with the psyche. The change is imperceptible as it loses touch with each momentary essence. It literally becomes a different person as personality is merely a manifestation of the ever-changing psyche.

Time travel is the isolation of a momentary essence causing a shift in focus to a particular block of memories, thus once again savouring the atmosphere of an almost forgotten moment. All possibilities coexist. As the free will chooses which one to experience it is recorded and stored.

Travelling into the future you only see probabilities based on the course taken by the psyche. The morbid psyche has no free will, hence no ability to plot a course according to pure reasoning. (*See* The Magic of Free Will).

Memories never fade. They are just pushed aside by the prevailing priorities of current data being ingested. A moment of high emotion magnifies the essence, making it more easily accessible. Visualisation is important. There are books on the subject of astral projection giving good methods for time travel. It is not just an idea dreamt up to sell comics. It is a reality. If you wish to partake, check the list of momentary aspects. Write out the key aspects on a pad by your bed. The rest is done mentally. Visualise yourself where you wish to be.

Each recalled aspect awakens the memories of others. It is possible to visit anywhere, anytime as all times and places are together in one moment. Apart from your personal memories everything else in creation is accessible also.

The Magic of Free Will

Free will is the origin of all creation. It has the ability to transcend everyday belief systems. Even if there was a fixed future the free will can change the seemingly unchangeable, thus creating an alternative future. Alas, there is no future to change, only the present. The concept of a fixed future is championed by those who do not want you to tamper with their plans for you. They are well aware of the nature of time and use it to their advantage. Every moment is a completely new beginning. Free will lives in this new beginning where anything is possible. There is always the possibility that even the most morbid psyche can awaken to the existence of free will and free itself from the yoke of slavery and the foolish notion of a fixed future.

Truth and Permanence

Truth is the greatest healer of all. One glimpse of truth instantly unmasks all the falsehoods which spring from the denial of that truth. You look out the window and see the rain falling. You hear it strike the window. You accept the fact that it is raining as a truth. You accept as a truth that the sun rises in the east. There is another truth, one which does not rise or fall but transcends all senses. That is absolute truth. When all in creation is spent and destroyed there remains that which cannot be spent or destroyed.

There are three knowable aspects in creation, the two extremes of joyous beauty and painful ugliness with a hinterland of confusion in between. Beyond all that there is a stable reality. In that reality there is no ugliness or confused hinterland, just the essence of infinite beauty which transcends all the known or imagined beauty in creation. Thought only sees transitory illusions. Thought itself is only a transitory blip, a fleeting experience.

The seeker looks beyond all transient conditions to find a stability which cannot be anything but permanent. The seeker will always find the truth and truth will always touch the seeker. Truth can never be known or understood by a psyche, or even a mind. In order to see the truth the mind must first end the manifestation of the psyche, then transcend itself in humility to become utterly silent. Only then can the truth be seen.

Veils

There are levels of consciousness. Each level consists of a range of vibrations within which the individual functions.

They speak of seven veils which separate the levels, but the only veil which concerns you is the one facing you now. However large the building may be you can only pass through one door or level of understanding at a time. Each level is beyond the understanding of the levels below. The lifting of a veil represents the realisation of a new level of understanding.

An individual on the physical level does not automatically access the spiritual realms by simply dying. They just take their karma with them in the astral level. However, individuals who have worked on raising their conscious vibrations may access spiritual realms while still occupying a physical body and on the death of that body, thus bypassing the veil of the astral.

You cannot seek heaven as it is infinitely beyond all comprehension. You can only seek a nameless truth by eliminating all the falsehoods.

What they refer to as heaven is infinitely beyond the vanishing point of ultimately refined vibrations. In that nothingness is heaven, infinitely beyond all concepts, beyond all the teachers with their white beards, white robes and endless lessons.

There are only two possible scenarios on the death of the physical body. You either enter the spiritual realm or remain in the astral realm. There is a clear divide or a veil between spiritual and astral realms. Physical life is simply a denser aspect of the astral or mental realm.

In the spiritual realm there is an absolute freedom which infinitely exceeds any concept created by the wildest imagination. At present you are trapped within an endless network of illusions which make up the astral realm. You are suffering from a lack of consciousness and are being held deliberately within the denser astral layers. You are at the mercy of a race of deceptive astral or thought entities whose sole aim is to prevent you from leaving the confusion and torment of these realms. These entities use every trick in the book to prevent you from attaining a level of consciousness which would enable you to bypass the veil of the astral and enter the spiritual realm.

These deceptive entities have trapped themselves within the astral by deciding eons ago to make this their comfort zone and emphatically turning their backs on truth, creating for themselves a reversal of reality. These entities are now feeding on your suffering by recycling your psyche again and again through the belief systems which effectively hold your psyche prisoner to the astral concepts of reincarnation and karma. (*See* Karma, Crime and Punishment.)

Violence

Violence is the noise needed by those in denial to drown out truth. In the confused psyche it is the temporary abandonment of discipline. The memory stays deep within where it festers and manifests as guilt. Thus it remains hidden until it is laid bare by the dawning of consciousness and the birth of conscience.

War

When you come across a planet plagued by endless savagery, you ask why. All those involved in this totally insane violence claim they are not to blame and only wish to live in peace.

It is patently obvious that certain sections of the population are only trying to defend themselves against unwarranted attacks by small belligerent groups. So you can now remove all innocents under attack from the equation.

This now leaves belligerent groups to offer an explanation for their activities. Every effect has a cause. Whenever there arises discord it is patently obvious the trouble has to be initiated by one individual. It only remains to pinpoint that individual. You work backwards from the base of the pyramid. There are many belligerent groups, each having a leader. These leaders are answerable to central leaders on the next level above. They in turn bow to the next level above. Each level is only answerable to the level above and so on to the apex and the head of the serpent.

So it is only a very tiny part of the planetary population which calls the shots. The ones at the top use psychological trickery to maintain the status quo and consequently their own power and riches. It is therefore in their interests to perpetuate the endless violence.

These devious individuals are in turn controlled by planted urges from the world of thought which controls the physical world. They are only answerable to the thought-forms on the astral level.

All the violence on the planet, and the astral thought-forms or demons are the two facing mirrors which perpetuate each other within the grand illusion. (*See* Demons and Human Suffering).

Your enemy lulls you into a false sense of security as it creeps up behind you. In order to forestall the possibility of rebellion the controllers have established from an early stage the false beliefs of religious, social and national pride. Subdivisions were created by stealth within these foolish belief systems as an extra precaution in case any particular belief became a united front in opposition to the very establishment which created it. Hence, all the worldwide so called religions of today. They are too busy fighting each other to evolve the courage or common horse-sense to realise they have a common enemy. As a result humanity can now be easily manipulated into attacking and destroying each other's bravest individuals. These orgies of insane violence are allowed to continue for long periods. The brave ones who die first are the very ones who would be the first to serve in a popular rebellion against the common worldwide oppressors.

Thus the ranks of the opposition are kept thinned out. When they are satisfied enough have been killed off – hey presto, they step in with a magical political solution while donning their sad masks and pinning medals on the broken bodies.

> Our brave young hero knows his mission well,
> To seek and bomb the enemy to hell.
> Between the drifting silver clouds below,
> He saw the little houses row on row.
> In his mind he saw his child asleep,
> Wrapped up in dreamland back across the deep.
> The evening's fine, the mission a success,
> Back to base and coffee in the mess.
> Flying homeward to the setting sun,
> Little did he know what he had done.
> Back below, a child about to die,
> Begged a tear-soaked doll to tell her why.
> The ending of a life that's just begun,
> They've stolen your tomorrow's little one.
> Then one day it dawned upon his mind,
> The suffering of loved ones left behind.
> Slaughtered innocents the world around,
> While warlords cower like rats below the ground.
> To earn the right to live among real men,
> He swore he'd never fly those planes again.
> Just a hired killer days before,
> At last a hero true for evermore.
>
> Starved of hope and dignity,
> There is one way out you see.
> Just sign here and follow me,
> Quick march left right hup two three.
> The sergeant has a friendly word,

Get back in line, you @*#@ing turd.
I'll show you how a robot feels,
Straighten up and snap your heels.
Shoulder arms, now strand at ease,
Prepare for slaughter overseas.
No more hunger, no more thirst,
If your target hits you first.
Someone just like you and me,
Starved of hope and dignity.

A fence made of lies between you and the truth,
To capture your mind and manipulate youth.
To kill off in wars those who threaten the state,
A gun, then a handshake and 'off with you mate.'
'Get your ass over there and get shot in the head.'
We just want your life, you won't mind, you'll be dead.
You can die with your boots on or just in your socks,
It won't really matter you'll fit in the box.
If we run out of boxes a bag will come later,
If we run out of bags you can stay in the crater.
It's nice of you to die for us,
Go now, please don't make a fuss.
Of slaves we have a surplus now,
o had an overseas powwow.
Over tea we did agree,
To cull each other's slaves you see,
We'll be told our side has won,
To make it all seem right my son.

What's left of the war-weary population will go along with anything just to escape the mass torture of war. During these periods of 'peace' the masses are systematically kept psychologically 'hanging by a thread' in a collective condition of doubt, worry, fear and suspicion. These periods of comparative peace are in truth no more than a countdown till the next cull is required and duly engineered. Immediately after they have devastated a targeted area of the planet they send in what they call N.G.O.s (non-governmental organisations). These so-called N.G.O.s are no more than a silent army of occupation, each one fitting neatly into the final agenda. The main fodder of these organisations are totally unaware how they are being used as a trojan horse by their ultimate controllers.

Until recent times humanity in general has been kept in ignorance of the never-ending wars continuing all over the planet. The predators circulated images of smiling children in those territories where they had murdered good leaders and replaced them with evil dictators supported by private armies of thugs to crush and torment the long suffering native inhabitants. Many millions of these unfortunates were being held in slavery while your local cinema showed pictures of a happy people in colourful dress on golden beaches or cheerfully giving their labour in idyllic sun-soaked fields of fruit. As you sipped your morning tea or munched your way through a banana you could almost taste their blissful joy in the flavour. Even though you were surrounded by misery it gave some comfort to be told that such happiness existed in other parts of your planet.

War is the ultimate form of deliberately created mass hysteria. The powers which control earth have a number of reasons for this. It can be a local quibble, a deliberate population cull, a large-scale conspiracy or a ploy to create mass human suffering for consumption in the mental or astral world. Mass unemployment is arranged to help recruit all the cannon fodder needed to supply the bloody fields of mass insanity. It now only remains to dress all those confused palookas in similar rags which are no more than prison garb, give them hard heels to slam together in cowardly obedience and dangerous weapons to play with. The arrogant imbecilic puppet with the three small rags on its shoulder is the sum total of the wind-up toys' brainpower as it barks at the ranks like a purple-faced Rottweiler.

A short period of concentrated brutalisation takes place just to discourage any humane thoughts. The order goes out; 'Quick march, kill as many of the ones in different coloured rags as possible before they stop you by enthusiastically redesigning your ass. It's a game. Go play it you goddamn heroes. If we think you lack enthusiasm we will make an example of you by sticking you against a wall and blowing your tonsils into the next country. Go-Go-Go.'

The ones making it back to the motherland have marvellous stories to tell their spawn. Those with missing parts push out their chests to display pieces of metal and animal hide they were given as a reward for having three A-levels in stupidity. This means they are fully qualified cannon fodder. They firmly believe they have done a service to their people. They have not.

They have served the elite agenda. War is the continuous supply of human suffering as a sacrifice to astral demons. A false sense of comradeship is instilled into the psyche of the palooka in order to create peer-pressure. This move ensures that the palooka will gladly die rather than lose face.

Put a uniform on them and they become that uniform, as the psyche is no more than a slave to its physical surrounds and identifies with what it is conditioned to see as authority. Because of this it will fearfully obey orders rather than risk disobedience.

In most cases this compliance is simply a blind unthinking conditioned response, but in some cases it can be abject cowardice when the individual realises a particular order should not be obeyed but still slavishly and shamefully complies. The demon of guilt is forever waiting in the wings and now hops aboard the suicide express.

The spineless one says, "I'm just doing my job." No, you are not just doing your job. Your real job is to act according to what your own mind tells you and not someone else's.

To be human is to know when to obey or not to obey an order. By blindly obeying an order you are making yourself not just the enemy of all good people but your own worst enemy.

Y

Yoga

Due to the mindless corruption of influential corporations, councils and the agendas of devious individuals, today's so-called societies are directed relentlessly and mercilessly against the individual's mental and physical well-being. You are very fortunate if you have a free mind capable of withstanding this onslaught. Inner discipline is needed more than ever to withdraw temporarily from the surrounding madness. It is important to keep contact with the balance of individual freedom of being. It is a sad fact that the alternative is to be caught up in the nonsensical mess and devoured by the insatiable greed of the machine.

The average person would consider many of the inner disciplines to be too fantastic or obscure to bother with in a life already seemingly full to capacity. This is understandable as the average psyche is choc-a-block with crass nonsense disguised as meaningful data. However, there are a few aspects which may be of interest to somebody. To the clear mind inner discipline is an integral part of the natural flow of life, but the psyche needs to be made aware of its existence and the capacity and need for change.

Yoga is just a word which can be applied to many disciplines of mind over body, mind over psyche or mind over mind. There is the sense of the unity of mind and body and the sense of total respect for all life. This infuses living with a real direction and meaning which transcends the mundane. As with every other positive aspect of living the concept of yoga has been hijacked by the clowns of chaos and converted into show business in order to take money from the gullible. Contrary to popular belief there is no need to twist your body into painful knots to achieve some kind of harmony or psychedelic rush. Discomfort is totally unnecessary and is not part of any meaningful discipline. True discipline is the understanding of life and the creation and maintenance of a ompletely relaxed, comfortable healthy life. There are many disciplines involved. The names given to them are not important. An accurate description of each process will suffice.

RELAXATION

How much of your day can you really call your own? Most people go through life without ever properly relaxing. They remain tense day and night, thus depriving themselves of true rest and regeneration. Think of the body as a spring. When a spring is stretched or compressed it creates tension. When slowly released it returns to its point of equilibrium or maximum state of rest. Cats are masters of posture and relaxation. All their movements are spring-like. They always stretch carefully before resting.

Put aside the cares of the day. After a good night's rest you can handle them from a better perspective. You can sleep curled up in a ball or flat out. It does not matter as long as you have stretched properly. Lie on your back, arms down by your sides. Become aware of your whole body inside and out. Slowly stretch your arms and legs till they have reached their maximum length. Then slowly relax them to return to their points of equilibrium. Never make sudden moves while exercising. It may cause strain or cramp. Visualise waves of white healing light passing through you from head to feet while washing away the tiredness. Become aware of a tingling it creates as it passes through. It enters your head as you inhale and leaves your feet as you exhale.

Deliberately relax every muscle in your body. You will discover there are many tense muscles you thought were relaxed. Concentrate on relaxing these. Give special attention to the neck and shoulders. Also relax the facial muscles leaving the face expressionless. As you do, your limbs will seem to become heavier. Visualise them becoming as heavy as lead and sinking into the bed. Feel the weight of your body pressing down. Then very slowly release this feeling of weight till you feel as though you could float away. Be aware of the tingling all over. This is the regeneration at work. With practice the whole process only takes a few minutes. Try to keep your back straight during the day. Never make demands on your body. Treat it with care and it will not let you down. If you don't treat your body like a spring you are dragging round a dead weight. When you rest, surrender completely to gravity, after all, you have been fighting it all day. Have respect for gravity as it is the controlling force in the physical world.

SLOW MOTION

The practice of slow motion has a beneficial effect on daily life both inwardly and outwardly. Make any sequence of movements, but slowed to about a tenth of the usual speed. Normally the psyche, (which thinks of itself as your mind) gives one second of attention (if that much) to one second of movement. If a particular movement has become fully automatic the psyche gives it no attention whatsoever. Slow motion forces the psyche to give at least ten times the usual attention to each movement.

It becomes aware of the intricacies involved. There can be a struggle to maintain balance but this becomes easier with practice. The result is that all the movements become deliberate actions which override the usual automation. This exercise improves balance and alertness while disciplining the psyche, preventing it from wandering. You will become much more aware of all your movements. All it takes is a few minutes each morning. The continued awareness of gravity maintains a spring like posture.

BREATHING

When you are at rest or sleeping, deep breathing is not necessary. You can practice the art of shallow breathing. Some adepts can stop breathing altogether for long periods. These are extremely advanced in the art but this kind of activity reduces the dignity of yoga to the level of a circus act. Although such things are possible there really is no need. Study your automatic breathing pattern. Become aware of how deeply you breathe and how much air is still in your lungs after you exhale. Try exhaling as much as possible without straining. Never strain yourself. Always hold back a little in everything you do. Doing so maintains a safety margin and stores vital energy. (*See* Yoga—Effort, Energy and Faith).

After you have expelled most of that remaining air, slowly inhale again. Do not gulp the air in. Only inhale as much as is necessary. As with the practice of slow motion you are becoming more aware. You can reduce your breathing till it is similar to a cat's pant. Don't worry about suffocating. You won't. During the day you can occasionally visualise the white light, inhale it deeply and hold it as long as is comfortable so you don't have to gasp when you exhale. This increases energy and physical strength. There are advanced exercises to do with breathing in and out of alternate nostrils but they are not relevant to everyday living. Discipline frees you from automation and even if forgotten, is never wasted.

VISUALISATION

In the pursuit of any new skill or craft there are many surprising aspects to be discovered. As your studies become more intense, each new territory entered leads to yet another. At times the going gets tough but you push your way through the bottleneck and the rewards give you a renewed zest. It is just so with the study of visualisation. Visualisation frees you from conditioning.

You may think what the eye, ear or hand cannot see, hear or touch does not exist. It does, and it's all out there. The world in which you find yourself is a created shell which forms the boundary of all thought. Inside this shell you have formed your own small personal shell which has become your comfort zone. Your whole life is contained in this small shell. Visualisation extends the boundaries of your world and can eventually break down the walls of your self-made prison.

Outside the comfort zone all possibilities exist. Seeing the nature and extent of these phenomena is limited only by the imaginative ability of the individual psyche. Visualisation is the concentrated focus of the imagination. It can lead to experiences far beyond physical consideration which cannot be described in words. When you think you are creating something new or unique in your imagination you are merely seeing what is already there.

The expansion of thought is only a means to an end, not an end in itself. With the expansion of thought the psyche can outgrow itself and your real inner identity can progress beyond thought and see reality. If you visualise a ball of white healing light it is already there. The physical senses can only handle so much data but imagination is that aspect of the psyche which can travel beyond the shell of the comfort zone and into uncharted waters. Some would have you believe that imagination is no more than a flight of fancy. This is not true. Imagination is every bit as real as anything which impacts on the senses. You must suspend your belief system as this is the stumbling block which holds back your journey through many amazing adventures and beyond into reality. You can risk all for the sake of truth. There is nothing to be afraid of. No harm comes to those who dare, only those who don't.

You can study any object large or small. It can be a building, a tree or a very small object. Begin with a small simple object. Study it for a minute. Shut your eyes and visualise it as perfectly as you can. Go over every detail. Note any discrepancies and keep trying till your visual memory is perfect. This exercise greatly improves your observation and gives you a photographic memory. Progress to more detailed objects. You can eventually study a tree for a few minutes at a time. If you persist you will be able to remember every branch and leaf just as you can remember every word and note of a song. It is time well spent if you can spare it.

The above example is the memorising of what your senses tell you is there. Creative visualisation is a different discipline. It is the sensitisation and development of the perception of those phenomena which the physical senses cannot detect. Visualisation has many uses. It is used in magic, and in conjunction with three other aspects it can injure or kill. As with anything else, it becomes a weapon in the wrong hands. It can be used also as a force for good. To abuse any ability would be a monumental error.

Visualisation can be used for controlling heartbeats, creating high-pitched sound which effects electronic equipment, telekinesis, astral projection, raising and lowering vibrations, transmitting sensations, spiritual and sexual melding, healing, time distortion, Kundalini, creating heat and cold and doing without trying. Only details of the simplest aspects will be given here for two reasons. Some are highly dangerous and others are too advanced to be described in words as they go beyond the limited concept of thought. Beyond these details given here it is up to the individual to progress to the more advanced disciplines.

ASTRAL PROJECTION

Astral projection has nothing to do with dreaming with the one exception of the lucid dream. In the case of the lucid dream you can leave the dream and journey in the astral or mental world. Astral projection is the conscious releasing of the mental body from the physical one. There are hundreds of books on the subject giving many methods. Many are complicated but the simplest ways are best.

Lie face down in bed. Turn your head to either side. You do not need to have your arms down by your sides. Just make sure you are completely comfortable. Visualise yourself lying on a warm beach with your feet pointing towards the sea. The sounds of the surf breaking along the shore and the odd seagull's cry are wafted in on the sea breeze. The warm breeze relaxes you as it caresses your body. Visualise the wave of relaxation moving up your body. You begin to go to sleep from your feet up. Here is the important part. Keep your head physically relaxed but your mind wide awake and alert. This is necessary for a conscious projection. If you allow your concentration to drift you will just go to sleep.

As soon as the wave of relaxation reaches your neck you float out of your body with the greatest of ease. You float through the walls of your house and you are on your way to wherever you wish. Try to keep calm, as your first success will probably shock you and you will shoot back into the physical. Have you ever awakened with a violent start? This is caused by the astral body slamming back into the physical. Don't worry about this. It is harmless. If there is a particular location you wish to visit use the same method and instead of slowly floating out of your body you will find yourself instantly at your destination. You will be invisible to others as your physical body is asleep where you left it. You can project any time day or night as long as your surrounds are reasonably quiet.

There are books which describe in detail experiences to be had in the astral realm. There are descriptions of astral time travel and how to achieve it. The possibilities are amazing. The ability to project is abused by governments, non-humans and perverts. Don't be tempted. The so-called military establishment refers to it as remote viewing and justifies it with that good old standby 'national security.' Read as many books on the subject as you can, a good read even if never used. In an ordinary dream you are at the mercy of the particular drama you find yourself in. In conscious projection you are the master of all you create. Don't believe any of this. Check it out for yourself. Bypass blind belief and make the knowledge your own.

DOING WITHOUT TRYING
Doing without trying is an act of faith. On the face of it this seems to be a contradiction in terms. Normally you would ask yourself how it was possible to do anything without at least trying. The concept is subtle, but perfectly logical. The truth is that trying to do something burns up vast quantities of vital energy. By trying, you lock yourself in a circle of negativity. You either do or don't. There is no middle ground. Trying presupposes the possibility of failure which becomes a subliminal negative. This creates inner conflict. All conflict dissipates energy. Having faith in yourself is not the same as believing or trusting in yourself. Faith has nothing to do with belief or trust. (*See* Faith, Hope, Charity and Trust).

There are numerous documented accounts of individuals having performed feats of super strength under certain conditions. Such individuals were merely bypassing their psychological barriers and tapping into their full natural human potential. Normally you tell yourself your abilities are limited, but in exceptional circumstances you go straight to the task without trying. This is because the alternative is unthinkable and you simply bypass your self-imposed limitations.

EFFORT AND ENERGY
If you begin a task by putting in 100% of your effort into it you leave yourself no reserves, either physically or psychologically. This is why you should always hold back a little in everything you do. If you approach that task with 50% effort you retain 50% reserve energy. Putting in 100% to begin with sets up a subliminal barrier to further resolve. Begin every task deliberately slowly. As your speed picks up you retain a high energy level without tripping over yourself. By beginning slowly and gradually speeding up you eventually complete the task more quickly and efficiently and still have energy to spare.

FORESTALLING NEGATIVE EVENTS
All your sensual awareness of perceptible creation is automatic. Everything is connected, even though you may not be aware of those connections. Your every thought and action is seen at all times, not only by the collective consciousness but by many shadowy and predatory aspects of the locally created illusion. Your thoughts are known by the vibrations emitted by your essence. Through introspection and discipline you can gain control of your own essence. You can change the nature of your emitted vibrations by visualising your psyche in a particular

situation caused by a negative event.

By recognising the possibility of a negative event you greatly reduce the probability of that event occurring. By transforming your essence into a state which emulates the condition of a psyche which expects such an event, you set up a psychic barrier. It is like finding out a lie, it is no longer effective. Your essence gives out the message that you are expecting the event in question, thus eliminating the element of surprise. All negative events need the element of surprise and turn their attention elsewhere in the face of the slightest difficulty or challenge. The reason why psychic tricks like this work is because of the totally automatic nature of the whole thought process. The more conscious or aware the mind or psyche is, the more easily it can disarm the automatic system.

VISUAL MEMORY
Randomly doodle on a sheet of paper while listening to a radio programme. It could be a discussion or a play. When the programme has finished look over what you have drawn. You will find that each detail will recall part of the programme. This shows how the sight and hearing are subliminally bound together. The effect is not as strong when listening to music as the psyche is more relaxed and prone to wander.

KUNDALINI
You do not set out with the intention of attaining new abilities or powers. The opposite is the case. There is never a question of any kind of reward when you begin the journey. Discipline involves a great deal of dedication, concentration and sacrifice. New abilities are a natural part of the process. Each discipline leads to a new ability which in turn leads to another discipline. Any discipline, from the viewpoint of a morbid psyche is simply a case of attempting to do the impossible, a complete nonsense and waste of time. Because of this attitude the morbid psyche would not for one moment consider self-discipline. A psyche must first rise above itself and break free from its own morbidity before it can enter the world of discipline.

This is just the beginning of a journey into a land where laws no longer apply and the individual's real true identity begins to re-establish itself. With real identity comes the return of original free will. It is not a case of learning. It is a case of unlearning and returning to the simplicity of nothingness. With the attainment of new abilities there is no sense of power, pride or smugness as such negatives have vanished in the quickly fading world of illusions. You leave thought behind as you enter new realms of amazing wonders and sensations.

Kundalini is the pinnacle of human endeavour. It is the greatest wonder of the physical world. It completely obliterates all negative thoughts in those nearby. It is the most awesome thing this side of heaven.

It is like a gentle fire in the presence of which everything else melts like ice. The beauty is unbearable as it literally takes your breath away. The physical aspect is a whooshing sensation emanating upwards from the seat of orgasmic essence behind the sex organs. It is as though the very core of your being is exploding and escaping through the spine and head. It is accompanied by a feeling of infinite elation which contains all possible human aspirations a million times over. It is the light which banishes every trace of darkness. Kundalini may be quite rightly described as a universal orgasm as heaven enters earth in the ultimate union of existence and non-existence.

THE PENDULUM METHOD FOR CONTROLLING RHYTHMS
Look at a clock pendulum. Visualise it swinging half an inch behind its actual position. Don't just visualise a separate pendulum but the actual pendulum itself as though your mind is pulling it back and forcing it to slow down. A pendulum can actually be slowed or stopped using this method. It depends on how strongly you have developed your willpower and visualisation. A serious determined state of mind is required. These are serious disciplines, not flippant party games. This particular practice is known as psychokinesis or mind over matter. To speed up the pendulum visualise it just ahead of itself.

The same method is used to control heartbeats. If you lie still you can feel the pulses in the brain. When the heart is held back for a couple of beats and suddenly released you can feel the extra surge of pressure in the brain as the first beat after release is much stronger than the usual pulse. If your heart ever skipped a beat you will be familiar with the phenomenon. This surge can be used in conjunction with Kundalini.

SONICS
The physical body is just a temporary vehicle, a clever mechanism. It is a part of the physical world and largely subject to its laws. The ear mechanism can be made to transmit as well as receive just as with any electrical device. Sit or lie quietly. Visualise a three inch ball of light energy in the centre of the brain. As well as visualising it make sure you can actually physically feel it. When you can feel it try extending it sideways to touch the inner mechanisms of the ears. When it touches, increase the energy level thus. As you inhale take in energy with the breath. As you exhale retain the energy and just release the breath. While you are exhaling, guide the saved energy into the brain, and so on. This exercise requires your divided attention as you must concentrate equally on the breathing and the guiding of energy. This has the effect of pumping up the energy in the brain.

If at any point the pressure in the brain becomes excessive simply stop building it up and it will die back to its normal level. Too much pressure can cause a headache. If you have no evil intent no harm will come to you. Rest assured of that. Eventually an extremely high-pitched whistling sound like a dog-whistle is produced. This effects electronic equipment while causing a very fine tingling and tickling sensation in the inner ears. Proceed very carefully.

DIRECTING ENERGY

Visualise a ball of energy in the brain. Try moving it around in the brain, circling to the right and left. When you are confident you have accomplished this move it outside to circle your head. Wherever it goes be aware of the feeling within it. Never proceed to the next stage till completely confident with the present one. Next move it away from you in a straight line and back again. Do this in every direction including behind you. You can eventually send it into someone's head with the required intention. Never forget the warning about abuse. The direction of energy can be used in many ways. It can be made to replicate any concept, emotion or sensation. All it requires is the perfection of the intention through practice.

INNER AWARENESS

Visualise the ball of white healing light in your brain. Proceed slowly. Move it down your throat and round inside your body. Become aware of every part of your insides. Note any aches or pains. Centre the energy in that location along with the intention to convert any harmful chemicals into gas. If successful, the resulting gas will be expelled from either end of the body. If the area is near the surface apply the gentle pressure of a thumb or knuckle.

The whole being must consciously work together with an equal awareness in every aspect, mental and physical. All aspects must work as a team. Those secret inner parts have laboured for years in your service while being ignored. Endow them with a life and awareness of their own in the same way you have endowed your hands with their own coordination and sensitivity.

MELDING

The psyche is usually so busy with its own projected images it is blind to incoming signals. It is a mental one-way traffic system. This causes conflict and division in society. It is possible to silence or neutralise the creation of projected images. The result is the full clear perception of incoming signals. The essence of another can be felt physically like a sheet of electronic currents. It is like the pull of a magnet. It is as though the absence of outgoing signals creates a vacuum which sucks in the essence of another. This is known as melding.

RAISING AND LOWERING VIBRATIONS

Music is created by varying wavelengths. The shorter or finer the vibrations the higher the notes. Every aspect of the physical world represents a particular note according to the rate of its vibrations. Think of your brain as a note. Your conscious mind knows which note that is. You will at some point have run through a tune mentally so you have the ability to visualise music in your brain. If you concentrate on sensing or 'feeling' the brain you will at some point become aware that it gives off a hum. This hum is more a feeling than an audible sound. This is your rate of vibrations. Being an advanced exercise, it requires great dedication.

When you feel the hum in your brain you can, through visualisation raise or lower the vibrations giving a higher or lower note. All beings including animals have their own individual hum. If you concentrate on an individual or animal while slowly raising or lowering your vibrations their head will give a little involuntary jerk as your rate momentarily coincides with theirs.

DOING THE IMPOSSIBLE

The psyche sets itself limits in every situation, physical or mental. This is the result of built-in misconceptions within the virtual reality machine you have come to accept as total reality. If you look closely at these limitations you will discover the exact point where the possible becomes the impossible. This point represents the edge of a precipice in the psyche which is normally a no-go area. The psyche is too frightened to venture near the edge. It is not until the psyche plucks up the courage to step over the edge that it discovers it is still on solid ground and the precipice was just an illusion instilled through a morbid fear of the unknown. You have challenged the deception and it has collapsed in a heap of dust to be blown away by the fresh wind of truth. That required courage depends on the overpowering selfless impulse to find the truth outweighing the morbid fear.

There are many more simple disciplines with immediate results which will not be disclosed here as they could be weapons in the wrong hands. As for the rest, the information given here is more than enough to enable a genuine seeker to advance beyond thought. Beyond that, the disciplines, abilities and temptations are ever greater till a point is reached where the identity is no longer subject to temptation and is beyond even the concept of discipline. It is now free and finally at rest while it observes all the movement around it. In this final human state there is a constant influx of energy with no expenditure whatsoever.

That Summer Morn.

Once into a free world born,
to wake up to a summer morn'.

To rise and shine and breathe the air,
and greet the day without a care.

The new day seemed to wish you well,
and somehow held you in its spell.

The flowers with a gentle sway,
would usher in another day.

The sun beamed through a misty haze,
another of those endless days.

Everything alive and bright,
would shimmer in the golden light.

Forgetting that you'd ever slept,
an age before the shadows crept.

A thrilling feeling in your heart,
so many choices, where to start.

Some to take and much to give,
a better way for all to live.

It took so little to survive,
it was great to be alive.

Hard these days to comprehend,
how such happiness could end.

But far away and out of sight,
some demons lived where day was night.

On that planet far away,
all the gold had turned to grey.

They seemed to take instead of give,
in constant fear they seemed to live.

On your planet they had spied,
long before their world had died.

So with nothing left to take,
they left a dead world in their wake.

Their careful blueprint now it seems,
was to rob you of your dreams.

To leave one dead world in their wake,
and another world to take.

So their evil plans they made,
your peaceful planet to invade.

A simple people in their power,
those martians crushed you like a flower.

A flower whose beauty was so bright,
the demons could not bear the sight.

Your hands and feet they could not bind,
so they crawled into your mind.

Now they've taken all they can,
they're set to make another plan.

The humans who escape their graves,
will then be taken off as slaves.

But once again there is a twist,
another in an endless list.

The final twist depends on you,
for you must choose between the two.

To leave a dead world in your wake,
or give a bit more than you take.

And cause a new day to be born,
and once again that summer morn'.

A Final Word

As stated at the beginning, the sole purpose of this manuscript is to point out some relevant facts regarding the human condition and show how it is possible to regain full consciousness. It is not an exercise in laying blame or pointing a finger in any direction, as ultimately all are one. The whole thing revolves around one important chapter. All the other chapters merely deal with side issues which become irrelevant after a study of the chapter on reawakening to full consciousness. Life should be an exhilarating experience not to be wasted in the service of fools. In a clockwork world of gyrating fools the awareness level is the soil in which the seed of consciousness may be planted. All the above is less than one tenth of the full comprehensive manuscript, the tip of the iceberg.

Many manuscripts have been carefully concocted in such a way as to suggest that the concepts of suffering, war, karma and monetary systems of control are morally acceptable. There are no 'buts' or 'exceptions' in absolute truth, no holy wars, no glib jargon, no promises or justification of suffering.

Those manuscripts also suggest that victims are themselves responsible for the suffering inflicted on them by the very authors of such manuscripts, the purpose of which is to counter absolute truth thus causing confusion and self-doubt among the masses. The fakes also criticize the old religions while in fact they themselves are 'the new religion'.

The purpose of all this chicanery is to give the impression of real change when in fact it is just a new mask to maintain the old timeless control system, a new door for the prison cell of the human psyche. They have learned that the black art of deception works best by stealth. They forever seek new ways to make the unacceptable appear acceptable. Thus they have stolen the very earth from beneath your feet. The time has come to take back control of your life and with it your sanity.

Further Reading

David Icke – A fearless investigator
J. Krishnamurti – A pure spirit
John Pilger – A man of conscience

www.ingramcontent.com/pod-product-compliance
Lightning Source LLC
Chambersburg PA
CBHW051546010526
44118CB00022B/2599